Ceremonial Costumes of the Pueblo Indians

Ceremonial Costumes of the Pueblo Indians

Their Evolution, Fabrication, and
Significance in the Prayer Drama

VIRGINIA MORE ROEDIGER

UNIVERSITY OF CALIFORNIA PRESS

BERKELEY LOS ANGELES OXFORD

UNIVERSITY OF CALIFORNIA PRESS
BERKELEY AND LOS ANGELES, CALIFORNIA

UNIVERSITY OF CALIFORNIA PRESS, LTD.
OXFORD, ENGLAND

Library of Congress Cataloging-in-Publication Data

Roediger, Virginia More.
Ceremonial costumes of the Pueblo Indians : their evolution, fabrication, and significance in
the prayer drama / Virginia More Roediger ; with a new introduction by Fred Eggan.
p. cm.
Reprint. Originally published: Berkeley, Calif. : University of California Press, 1941.
Includes bibliographical references.
ISBN 0–520–07630–3. — ISBN 0–520–07631–1 (pbk.)
1. Pueblo Indians—Costume and adornment. 2. Pueblo Indians—Rites and ceremonies.
3. Pueblo Indians—Dances. 1. Title
E99.P9R6 1991
391'.0089974–dc20   91–18427
                                                           CIP

9 8 7 6 5 4 3 2

The paper used in this publication meets the minimum requirements of American National Standard
for Information Sciences—Permanence of Paper for Printed Library Materials, ANSI Z39.48–1984.
∞

PREFACE

AN IMAGINARY TIME MACHINE *is not the only instrument by means of which we may be carried into the past. The past lies near to our doors if only we will open our eyes and take notice of it. Amid the mechanical wonders and terrors of this generation cultural relics exist which have been passed down from age to age relatively unaltered since first the continent of America was discovered, explored, and colonized. In the homes of the Pueblo Indians of New Mexico and Arizona part of man's history is enshrined.*

A good deal of archaeological and ethnological research has been expended upon the lives of these Indians, but more still is needed—needed especially in these days when modern methods are threatening to shatter age-old customs. The Indian culture survived the missionary methods of Franciscan friars from Spain; nominal acceptance of Christ and the Virgin did not in any respect alter or prohibit the celebration of more ancient ceremonials. But the present-day school is proving more effective than the Catholic chapel and what could not be accomplished by the preacher the teacher is easily doing. There is unquestioned danger that this antique culture may, in a few years, vanish utterly.

Because of this, Miss Roediger's survey is of supreme importance. A student of the theater, she has realized that the theater embraces more than Broadway, that in the dances of the Pueblo Indians there resides an essential dramatic quality which has value both intrinsically and historically as a living example of those cultural roots from which the modern tragedy, comedy, and problem-play have sprung. In this volume she has endeavored, by a combination of personal field work and of careful examination into all available published records, to describe and explain the dance dramas still to be seen in the pueblos. Rightly, she has recognized that merely general descriptions are not sufficient, and perhaps the greatest significance of her work has been her attempt to demonstrate in detail the various aspects of her subject. She has not remained satisfied with outlining the appearance of a costume; from the finished dress she carries us back in an exact account of the cloth used, of the method of dyeing, and of the processes of manufacture. The movements of the dancers are related to their religious conceptions, to their secret ceremonies in the kivas, and to their methods of training. Just such a study as this was needed. I for one welcome it heartily and I feel sure that I shall not be alone in giving it this welcome.

ALLARDYCE NICOLL

AUTHOR'S PREFACE

IN AN ANALYTICAL *survey of costumes which have been for centuries the ceremonial raiment of a particular group of people one must also set forth those distinguishing traits of the group which have developed through environment and heritage, with whatever coloring has resulted from the external influence of encroaching foreign cultures.*

The dramatic instinct is an inherently human trait. It is conspicuous in the lives of even the lowest savages. Its first manifestation is the desire to dress for an occasion of worship. The worship generally takes the form of a prayer expressed in action, which is an attempt through the potency of costume and ceremony to coerce or solicit the interest of the spirits who supposedly have made themselves felt in the forces of nature and whom primitive man conceives of as a pantheon of supernatural powers. The spirits possess the secrets of the perplexing problems of life and death, and must be approached through supplication, compulsion, or sorcery.

I have selected the Pueblo Indians of Arizona and New Mexico because they are an outstanding example of a native culture still existent and for that reason deserving of generous and detailed investigation. Moreover, in my opinion, they are the most advanced of any native community in all North America in the perfection of dramatic-religious costumes. I here present a full and compre-hensive account of the characteristics of this dramatic-religious dress as it evolves from their geographical location, their mode of life, and their beliefs and manifestations—those elements of their civilization to which they have clung despite several hundred years of corruption and suppression by the white man. I have attempted, by word and sketch, to build up a picture of the cere-monial costumes which have resulted from this civilization.

There are not many more years during which it will be possible to make such a study. The decline has already set in and the contemporaneous state of Pueblo culture is one of decay and disintegration.

V.M.R.

INTRODUCTION

VIRGINIA MORE ROEDIGER'S *Ceremonial Costumes of the Pueblo Indians: Their Evolution, Fabrication, and Significance in the Prayer Drama* was first published in 1941 and reprinted, with black-and-white illustrations, in paperback two decades later. It soon went out of print. The reappearance of the classic original edition in full color is a welcome event.

The view of ritual and ceremony as a dramatic performance, currently fashionable in anthropology, was pioneered by Dr. Roediger in the 1930s. As a student of drama at Yale University, she was encouraged by Dr. Leslie Spier, then in the newly established Department of Anthropology and Linguistics, to study the costumes and dances of the Pueblo Indians found in museums and photographic collections and observed in the Pueblo villages of the Southwest during the mid-1930s. A student of drama, she was naturally interested in what went on "backstage" in the kivas and ceremonial rooms. Although there were restrictions on visitors even then, the dancers in their costumes could be seen in action in the plaza performances, and the construction of the costumes could be examined in museum collections and elsewhere.

Ceremonial Costumes of the Pueblo Indians is a book of value to a variety of people. It will be appreciated by the layperson or tourist who sees a Pueblo dance in one of the villages. It will also aid the technical historian and the scholar because of its careful research and clear descriptions. It will be particularly useful to the curatorial staff of the museum world, and to the new exhibit staffs that are increasingly being employed in larger museums.

The illustrations are beautifully done, since the author is both an artist and a scholar—the twenty-five line drawings and the forty full-color plates both illuminate the text and dramatize the subject matter. In an introduction to the original edition, Dr. F. W. Hodge, then the director of the Southwest Museum, Los Angeles, wrote:

Roediger's book presents more than its title connotes. For not only are the evolution, fabrication, and significance of Pueblo costumes discussed, together with the body paint, dance paraphernalia, and other appurtenances, but by way of background, the history and present life of the Pueblos are summarized in all their ramifications, and the significance of the ceremonies in which they play a living part is likewise discussed. No researcher among the Pueblo Indians will fail to give this volume his hearty recommendation.

The background information on the Pueblos and the language used in describing them are, of course, dated in many respects, since archaeologists and social anthropologists have learned a great deal since the 1930s. The Basket Makers, for example, are now seen as the direct ancestors of the Pueblo peoples rather than as a separate group, and archaeologists have developed a more complex ancestry for the whole Southwest. After an early period when Stone Age hunters killed large Pleistocene mammals at water holes and elsewhere, changing climatic conditions brought in modern flora and fauna and new populations of hunters and gatherers known popularly as the Desert Culture and technically as the Desert Archaic.

In central Mexico agriculture gradually developed and spread northward as well as to the south. It was adopted early in the Christian Era by the Cochise peoples along the border of what is now New Mexico and by the Hohokam of southern Arizona. Further north, the Basket Makers—

hunters and gatherers—first adopted maize, or corn, and then pottery from the south, gradually settling down in agricultural communities that developed into the modern Pueblos. During the Pueblo period most of these populations gradually merged or became extinct. Today, they are generally known as the Anasazi, a Navajo word for "ancient ones."

Despite the superseded background and language, the core of Dr. Roediger's volume—the materials used in the costumes and their detailed analyses—is as relevant today as it was a half-century ago. Here we find the manufacture of cloth, the use of feathers and evergreens, the preparation of decorative materials, and their use in the production of garments, ornaments, and masks for a variety of costumes—mostly kachina figures from Hopi and Zuni and animal dance costumes from the Rio Grande region, where the masked dancers are not seen by outsiders. Leslie Spier, one of Dr. Roediger's mentors, wrote that "there is no other book on Pueblo ceremonial costume that is so complete . . . and adequate in its descriptions," and in 1940, a year *before* its publication, he noted how valuable the manuscript was in staging the scenes of the Coronado Entrada pageant in New Mexico.

In her final section Dr. Roediger is concerned with the use of costumes in relation to the "prayer drama" and sees Pueblo worship as taking the form of a prayer expressed in action in the kachina dance. The cult of the kachinas is a central feature of religious activity in most of the Pueblos, and it is still possible to see masked kachina dancers in the western Pueblos of Zuni and Hopi, though the Spaniards forced such dances underground in their efforts to convert the Pueblo populations in the Rio Grande region. Here, social dances such as the Saint's Day Corn Dances, Buffalo Dances, and Animal Dances may be seen by visitors— they have costumes similar to those of the masked dancers, as well as similar choreography and songs. In the west the Hopi villages have masked kachina dances from the winter solstice to late July, when the Niman, or Homegoing Dance, sends the kachinas to their homes in the

San Francisco peaks; and the Zunis have kachina dances at various times throughout the year, culminating in the Shalako performances of December, in which ten-foot-tall masked figures dance all night, accompanied by various kachina groups and koyemci clowns, before returning to their homes in the Sacred Lake and elsewhere. Of the kachina dances, it has been said that "here is the best round of theatrical entertainment enjoyed by any people in the world, for religion and drama are here united."

For the Hopi, at least, the "prayer dramas" that Dr. Roediger envisaged as the central feature can be extended to most features of daily and ritual life. Individuals make prayer offerings throughout the year for their crops, their animals, and their relatives, but the major offerings are in the dances and ceremonies. There is still much to learn about the Pueblo peoples, but Dr. Roediger has shown us the way.

FRED EGGAN

Professor Emeritus, University of Chicago

CONTENTS

PART THREE: DETAILED ANALYSES OF PARTS OF COSTUMES

PART FOUR: COSTUMES IN RELATION TO THE PRAYER DRAMA

ILLUSTRATIONS

PLATES

NOTE ON PRONUNCIATION OF INDIAN WORDS AND PHRASES

SINCE THE LANGUAGE of the Pueblo Indians is not a written language, all attempts to select or contrive written symbols for it are arbitrary, and linguists differ in the symbols they prefer. The spellings used in the present work are intended to put the reader to as little trouble as possible; the words are to be pronounced about as they look, as, for example, kachina: *ka chi' na,* the middle syllable accented, the *ch* as in *church* and the *i* as in *machine.* In Tümas, Tungwüp, and Ahül the *ü* indicates a sound about like that of *u* in *church.* Accentuation is as follows:

A ho' li	Sai ya ta' ca
A hül'	Sa li ma pi' ya
Ka chi' na	Sha' la ko
Ko' ko chi	Shi pa' pu
Ko' yem shi	Shi' wan na
Ma' kwan pi	Si' o Sha' la ko
Pa' wi ka	Ta chu' ki
Po wa' mu	U' po yo na

PART ONE

The Pueblos, Their History and Present Life

THE TWENTY-SIX PUEBLOS, or urban homes, of the most interesting of all North American Indian communities lie in the region described by an arc curving southward from Black Mesa, in the arid plateau lands of the upper Colorado River basin of northwestern Arizona, to the flat banks of the clear waters of the Rio Grande, which flows from the mountains on the New Mexico–Colorado border. Here, on a shelf of land lying between the mountains to the north and the rough country which drops away to the south, on mesa and mound, by rain-lake and stream, are built in storeyed heights around central plazas the adobe brick and stone houses of these supposedly primitive people.

HISTORY

After careful research, the archaeologist has been able to reconstruct much of the past life of these Pueblo peoples. Culture periods, known as Basketmaker I, II, and III, the dates of which are undetermined, give us definite facts about a race of longheaded (dolichocephalic) men and women who populated the mesas and canyons of the Southwest. In Basketmaker I these people subsisted on game, seeds, and berries. They led a nomadic life and were sheltered by caves in the edges of the mesas. They used clubs and stone knives, and they made coiled baskets and twined and woven bags and sandals. In Basketmaker II they began to cultivate a kind of corn and a kind of squash, and to provide safe storage spaces they dug

[1]

pits in the floors of their caves. In Basketmaker III a sort of pit house was built, a shallow excavation covered with brush. Beans and several species of corn were grown and clay pottery was made. The bow and arrow appeared for the first time and feather robes replaced the previously worn robes of fur.[1]

About the time of Christ a new race of people appeared in the North American Southwest and drove the Basketmakers from their strongholds. The bones of these direct ancestors of the Pueblo Indians are recognized by their round (brachycephalic) heads and artificially flattened skulls.

Pueblo I (*ca.* A.D. 1–*ca.* A.D. 500) saw the building of permanent houses of several rooms on the surface of the ground. The turkey was domesticated and its feathers were used in clothing. Wild cotton was cultivated, spun, and woven into cloth—an industry destined to change the material culture of the area. Pueblo II (*ca.* 500–*ca.* 900) is believed to have known the organization of a definite clan system. Each group had its own house, which consisted of a number of one-storey rooms built around a court. In this period the kiva, or subterranean ceremonial chamber, became the central element in community life. Pueblo III (*ca.* 900–*ca.* 1300) has been called the Great Period or Golden Age of the prehistoric Pueblos. The remains of large community buildings still stand as mute testimony to the group life that existed within their walls. It was the early part of this period which beheld the highest development of the cliff dwellings and the many-roomed walled towns which were built on the mesa tops and in the valleys. There was also a high development in the arts and the material crafts. Pueblo IV (*ca.* 1300–*ca.* 1700) saw the breaking up of the large centers and a migration to sites with which the present-day pueblos correspond very closely. It was in this period that the historical records of Pueblo life were begun.

In 1540 Francisco Vásquez de Coronado led an expedition of discovery and conquest into this new country from which had come rumors of

---

[1] For numbered notes (references only) see pages 239–244, below.

the "Seven Cities of Cíbola," fabulously rich in gold and precious stones. Instead of the great riches they expected, the Spaniards found self-sustaining communities of natives. They called these communal groups *pueblos,* the Spanish word for villages. Exploration and subjugation were extended from the Colorado River as far as eastern Kansas. The locations of seventy pueblos were reported; many are occupied today.

The invasion followed soon after a great drought and the two calamities hastened the disintegration of the native civilization and forced the villages to consolidate. Forty years later, in 1581, history records that a party set out under the leadership of Fray Agustín Rodríguez to convert the heathen and explore the country. At the end of two years no word had been received from these soldier-priests: they had met an untimely death at the hands of their intended converts. A small expedition under Antonio de Espejo started north to trace its predecessor. Luxán, one of the party, wrote of their arrival among the Hopi: "Hardly had we pitched camp when about one thousand Indians came, laden with maize, ears of green corn, pinole [corn meal], tamales, and firewood, and they offered it all, together with six hundred widths of blankets, small and large, white and painted, so that it was a pleasant sight to behold."[2]

In 1598 Juan de Oñate attempted to colonize the country, and several communities of Mexican and Spanish settlers sprang up along the Rio Grande. By 1630 most of the pueblos had priests and churches. A period of suppression and of contention between civil and ecclesiastical authorities followed, and at the same time a resentment began to grow against the foreigners. The resentment flared into revolt in the Pueblo Rebellion of 1680. The result was the driving out of all Spaniards and the supremacy of native power for a period of twelve years. However, since no Pueblo Indian had the imagination to mold all the community groups into a strong nation, the rebel natives were at the mercy of the forceful and determined Don Diego de Vargas, who started north in 1692 and within a few months accomplished Spanish reoccupation.

Pueblo V (*ca.* 1700 to the present) finds the Indian permanently under the domination of a stronger power. Spanish rule ended in 1821, at the same time that Mexico threw off the yoke of Spain. There followed a period of trade. Santa Fe was at the western end of the covered-wagon trail and here the native Indian came into contact with commerce and the outside world. When the war between Mexico and the United States ended in 1848, the Treaty of Guadalupe-Hidalgo gave New Mexico to the latter country. As a territory belonging to a stable government, New Mexico gained peace. But what of the Indian? His free and open country has been replaced by small grants of impoverished land. The 'superior' and meddlesome white man has endeavored to arrange his life, judge his morals, and instruct him in a new civilization. Outwardly the Pueblo Indian has accepted the American's blue shirt and overalls, his canned peaches and coffee, but inwardly he remains aboriginal. The heritage of his race descends through him unmarred by the surface irritations of this 'higher' civilization. On his picturesque sites overlooking magnificent vistas of Arizona desert and New Mexican plain, he still lives a community life of peace and serenity that is his own. Or at least this has been so for a longer time than one might have hoped.

LOCATION OF PUEBLOS

Hopi.—In the extreme western end of the Pueblo country, in northern Arizona, the Hopi villages are perched on spurs and promontories with precipitous walls and limited level spaces, seven thousand feet above sea level. Situated much as they were when first seen by the Spaniards, they are divided geographically into three groups. To the east on First Mesa are the towns of Walpi and Sichomovi and the Tewa town of Hano; on the middle or Second Mesa are Mishongnovi, Shipaulovi, and Shungopovi; and to the west on Third Mesa are Oraibi and its two offsprings, Hotevilla and Bacabi. Although a growth of piñon and juniper on the

PLATE 1. *Zuñi woman in traditional dress.*   >>>→

Plate 1

mesa indicates rainfall sufficient for crops, the declivity of the land makes drainage so rapid that the rains are of little value. Nevertheless, there are springs and natural underground reservoirs which, with seepage and slow drainage, make agriculture possible in the valleys and washes.

Zuñi.—To the south and east, on the desert of western New Mexico, is a strip of land roughly following the course of the Zuñi River from its headwaters near the Continental Divide to a point near the Arizona border. From rugged forested mountains slashed by canyons there opens up to the south and west a wide, flat valley some six thousand feet above sea level. Through it the Zuñi River floods or trickles. Melting snow in the mountains or a sudden summer storm may within a few minutes transform the stream into a raging torrent which, subsiding, leaves silt and mud on its otherwise sandy banks. In the bordering hillsides to the east are perpetual springs of clear water. On a rise of ground west of the river, and in the center of the broad valley, is the principal town of Zuñi. It is surrounded by sandy flats on which is an indigenous growth of sage, greasewood, yucca, and small cacti. With care, the fields can be flooded and cultivated to raise the crops which are so essential to the life of these people. On near-by mesa, cliff, and plain are the ruins of former villages, the study of which proves that the "Seven Cities of Cíbola" which inspired the Coronado expedition of 1540 did actually exist—in whole or in part.[3] Today Zuñi is the sole urban unit, with the exception of four small summer settlements for the cultivation of distant fields.

Rio Grande.—The remaining pueblos are found on the eastern slope, across the Continental Divide. They are grouped along the Rio Grande and its tributaries, all of which flow southward from the wooded and canyoned foothills of a three-sided watershed. To the west are the Jemez Mountains; to the north, the Sangre de Cristo; and to the east, the Sandia and Manzano ranges. Here, where the low-banked streams are fringed with cottonwood and willow, lie broad flats of cultivable land which provide ample agricultural areas for the needs of the adjacent villagers. With an average elevation of fifty-five hundred to six thousand feet, these towns vary little in altitude from the pueblos farther west, but because of their accessibility, their proximity to the plains on the east, and their own diversified but closely related cultures these eastern groups present a complicated problem.

In order to understand the cultural relationships more clearly, it will be necessary to examine the linguistic affiliations.* These most definitely divide the villages.

The Hopi, of the west, are of Shoshonean stock and use a dialect of that branch of the Uto-Aztecan linguistic family. Zuñi has an individual language. The eastern groups, however, are of two linguistic units, the Keresan and the Tanoan. Because of their proximity to each other and the gradual infusion of outside influences it is impossible to classify with the linguistic affiliation the resultant habits and practices.

First, there are the seven Keresan-speaking pueblos:

Acoma.—A fortified town on the top of a precipitous mesa four hundred feet above the surrounding plain, on the southernmost edge of the Pueblo span, close to Zuñi.

Laguna.—Somewhat to the north and east, on the high north bank of the San José River, but nearer Acoma than any of the other pueblos.

San Felipe.—On the west bank of the Rio Grande, near the mouth of the Jemez River.

Santa Ana and *Sia.*—Both on the north bank of the Jemez River, respectively twelve and twenty miles from its mouth.

Santo Domingo.—On the east bank.

Cochiti.—On the west bank.

Both Santo Domingo and Cochiti lie farther up the Rio Grande Valley.

Then there are the eight Tanoan pueblos, the sites of which, curiously enough, almost enclose the Rio Grande Keresans, as may be seen by the map on the opposite page.

---

* See Appendix, p. 235.

Isleta and *Sandia*.—On the west and east banks, respectively, situated far to the south of the Keresan group on the Rio Grande. These pueblos form the southern division of the Tigua.

Jemez.—On the Jemez River above Santa Ana and Sia and below the mouth of San Diego Canyon.

Nambé and *Tesuque*.—To the east on two small tributaries, the Nambé and Tesuque rivers, a few miles north of Santa Fe.

San Ildefonso.—On the east bank of the Rio Grande.

Santa Clara.—On the west bank.

San Juan.—Farther north on the east bank.

The five last named form a group of towns on the sand dunes and plains occupied by the Tewa division of the Tanoan stock. The Hano, of the First Mesa of the Hopi, are emigrants from these.

Finally there are:

Picuris.—At the foot of the Picuris Mountains.

Taos.—The most northern of the pueblos, on both sides of the Taos River.

These two pueblos form the northern division of the Tigua.

CLIMATE

In general these varied groups of people live in a high, semiarid country watered by winter snows, sudden summer showers, and rivers from the mountainous north. Here, also, the southwest trade winds drop their moisture throughout the year. However, moisture is much needed in midsummer—by late July and August. It is at this time that the greatest activity is apparent among those cults whose duty it is to produce rain. The climate, on the whole, is healthful and invigorating. The temperature is fluctuating: intense heat of the summer day is mitigated by cool nights, and the hardship caused by the few winter storms is more than alleviated by the many days of unbroken sunshine. It is thus possible to spend much time out of doors.

SOCIAL CUSTOMS

The Pueblo Indians stand out sharply from other culture groups of North America. They have an urban existence and consequently have developed sedentary habits. They live indoors, rise late, and stay up on winter nights and gossip. Their entire life is influenced by their almost complete dependence upon agriculture for their food supply. Even their architecture is predetermined by the necessity of storage rooms for the harvest. The destructive forces of nature must be controlled, they believe, by magic, and the maturing of the crops is due to a pantheon of all-powerful spirits, including the Sun, the Earth, the Wind, and the Clouds.

Their permanent homes allow room for storage of produce, clothing, and sacred ceremonial paraphernalia. Compared with other semipermanent or roving peoples, they are rich in worldly goods. However, their concern is with tribal unity and not with personal prestige. Their lives are thoroughly formalized and highly ritualized, and they are greatly influenced by what we call superstitions. "Despite centuries of white contacts, they preserve their native culture perhaps more completely than any other Indian group in North America. Particularly is this true of their religious life, about which the eastern Pueblos . . . have built up an almost impenetrable wall of secrecy."[5]

ARCHITECTURE

The pueblo town is like a living organism; it is always being built and always being repaired. It may be a group of houses built in a pyramidal pile enclosing courts and plazas, as at Zuñi; or it may be built in two units, one on either side of a river, as at Taos; or again, it may be built in parallel lines, as at Acoma.

These flat-roofed houses are built together and on top of each other to the height of two or more storeys. The roofs are open paths from one neighbor's door to the next. Formerly, the entrance to the ground-floor room was a hatchway in the roof through which a ladder projected. There was no other opening, and the smoke was obliged to find its way out through this hole. The plaza, the center of all activity, was reached by descending a movable ladder which was drawn up in times of danger. The inner rooms of the houses were used for the storage of corn, other foods, and ceremonial equipment. Only members of the family might

FIGURE 1. Taos.

enter these chambers. Nowadays, there are doors and windows in all the outside rooms, and hooded fireplaces with chimneys.[6]

The building material used in the western pueblos is mostly stone, held together with adobe mortar and the whole covered with adobe plaster. In the east an unmolded adobe brick is used. The floor is usually packed earth, although it is sometimes paved with slabs of stone. The roof beams are of cottonwood, pine, or spruce, with cross poles covered with brush and earth. Within recent years modern tools and modern transportation have made it possible to build larger rooms, because longer timbers to serve as roof beams can be brought from the distant places—forested mountains—where they are procurable.

The heavy work of building is done by the men, but the women do all the plastering and finishing. It is customary, at least once a year, to do all necessary replastering, both inside and out, and to mend the holes and washes made by the heavy rains.

AGRICULTURE

Corn is the basis of Pueblo economic life. Various seed and melon plants are now grown, but corn, beans, squash or pumpkin, some varieties of gourds, the sunflower, and a kind of cotton were aboriginal. Other plants were introduced by the Spaniards and the Mexicans. Planting was done in April and May. The Hopi have a series of nine specified plantings, determined by the sunrise, between mid-April and June.[7] The Indian believed that planting must be done at a certain phase of the moon; for example, a waning moon was thought to have a bad influence upon the growth of plants.

Corn is the staff of life and the center of ceremony. Seed corn is kept two years so that in the event of a dry season there will always be enough for another planting. The corn is quick-growing and drought-resisting. It is planted deep, in irregular hills; often it depends upon seepage or underground water to quicken it into life. Colored strains of corn have been cultivated by the Pueblos for centuries, and the colors have ceremonial significance. A special blue corn is planted in May for the town chief of Cochiti.[8] A central place in myth and legend is given to the Corn Maidens, and the various colors of the grain are related to the directions. "The Tewa recognize seven varieties with the corresponding color directions of association and personifications. They are the following:

Blue corn, north	Blue Corn Maiden
Yellow corn, west	Yellow Corn Maiden
Red corn, south	Red Corn Maiden
White corn, east	White Corn Maiden
Many-colored corn, above	Many-colored Corn Maiden
Black corn, below	Black Corn Maiden
Dwarf corn, no direction	Dwarf Corn Maiden"[9]

PLATE 2. *Kachina doll, carved, painted, and decorated to represent a Sio Shalako from Hopi. Such representations of the supernaturals acquaint the children with the many powerful Beings who aid and protect them.* ⋙→

Plate 2

Fields are often owned by clans, as among the Hopi, or individually by the men and women, as in the east. The men work the fields, the women occasionally helping with the planting, and the entire family joins in the harvest. Communal labor is employed in certain fields and the crops from these are given to the town chief. This august person does not work, but spends his time in meditation on matters which are supposed to be for the good of the community.

Wild seeds and plants were formerly used for food. These included piñon nuts, acorns, juniper berries, yucca fruit, and many cacti. Certain plants and herbs still provide flavoring, and from others are obtained colors and adhesive gums used for dyeing materials and decorating masks.

In former days another major activity of the Pueblos was hunting, for the obtaining of food and skins. The hunting societies were influential; their leaders still hold active office in the round of ceremonial life.

POTTERY

Clay pottery is made by hand without the use of a potter's wheel.[10] The larger vessels are for water and storage. The cooking is done in crude, undecorated pots which serve only a practical purpose, but the water jars and the bowls used for serving food or for ceremonials are delicate in form and beautiful in design. The shapes, the use of colors, and the decorative motifs differ with the various localities.

DRESS

Before the Spaniards came, the men's dress consisted of soft-tanned deerskin or woven cotton. There might be a shirt, a breechclout, a kilt, and a robe of rabbitskin strips and, at an earlier period, a feather mantle. Leather moccasins or yucca-fiber sandals were used. The women wore a garment made of a rectangular piece of cloth wrapped around the body, fastened over the right shoulder, and sewed up the right side (pl. 1). Thus the left shoulder and arm remained bare and free. A long, wide belt was wrapped several times around the waist. A square of cloth, with two corners knotted under the chin, was allowed to hang down the back. Most of the time the women wore no foot covering, although long, wrapped moccasins of soft deerskin were worn on occasion. In the cold Taos country, snowshoes were worn in winter; elsewhere the feet were protected from snow by a piece of fresh deerskin with the hair side inward.

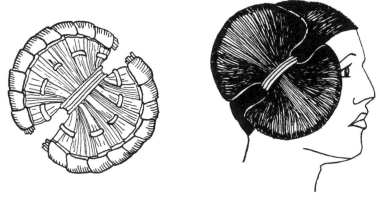

FIGURE 2. Hair dressed in side whorls worn by a maiden as a sign of virginity.
An old-style form made of cornhusks supplied the base of the butterfly shape.

Today—aside from the American store clothes—the men's dress is reminiscent of the Spanish Colonial period, modified, of course, by years of influence. The women retain their aboriginal dress, which is now worn over an undergarment.

Hair arrangement.—The long, black hair of both men and women is often queued, doubled over itself, and bound with a band at the nape. The sides are cut even with the ear lobe, and sometimes the women's hair is banged to the eyebrows. In some dances the hair hangs to the chin, simulating a mask or the Oriental veil (pl. 10).[11] The Hopi matron's hair is parted and gathered in two locks over the ears. "Each lock is wound over the first finger and the end drawn through as the finger is withdrawn."[12] The upper end of the lock is then wound with hair cord. The unmarried Hopi girls twist their long side and back hair on great eight-inch whorls which are worn over their ears to suggest the butterfly, the symbol of virginity. At Taos the man's hair is parted in the middle and allowed to hang on each side of his face in a braid or roll wrapped with yarn.[13]

COMMUNAL LIFE

There is little or no individual life within the pueblos. Work, play, and religious rites are group activities prompted by communal needs and aspirations. At designated times the crops are planted and harvested by working parties.[14] Houses, fences, and irrigation ditches are built by a man and his immediate family, and all who constitute his blood relations may be called upon to work together. Games are played by individuals and between tribal units which also participate in religious ceremonies. These ceremonies are directed in a stipulated pattern by various groups of men who have inherited or gained the positions of leadership. In the daily and yearly routine "they have hardly left space for an impromptu individual act in their closely knit religious program. If they come across such an act they label the perpetrator a witch."[15] Ruth Bunzel, speaking of Zuñi, says: "The supernatural, conceived always as a collectivity, a multiple manifestation of the divine essence, is approached by the collective forces of the people in a series of great public and esoteric rituals."[16]

The groups with which an individual may be associated are determined by birth, adoption, marriage, or election. The matrilineal exogamous clan system of the Hopi-Zuñi divides the villages into a series of named groups to one of which a child belongs from birth. This means that a child inherits its clan membership from its mother and must marry outside that clan. The clans establish the family line of descent in respect to certain official capacities in connection with other groups or cults. There are also strong clan systems in Acoma, Laguna, among the Rio Grande Keres, and even at Jemez. Farther east, among the Tewa, they become more and more feeble until finally, with the Tigua of Picuris and Taos, there are no clans at all. Strangely enough, Isleta has a pseudo clan division, following the east. Conversely, there appears the moiety, a more or less patrilineal division of the town into two parts, with a tendency toward endogamy (marriage within the group) fully developed among the Tewa.

"This division of the pueblo into two parts, or moieties, has usually been described in connection with social organization. It is true that it looms as large in the consciousness of the western pueblos, but it has no relation to the social organization . . . and . . . is evidently a ceremonial device associated with the kiva and with rain and fertility functions."[17]

"In the west the women own the houses, in the northeast the men, a mixed system of ownership prevailing in the towns between. In the west there are an efflorescent mask cult and an elaborate service of prayer-sticks or prayer-feather offerings, which diminish steadily to the east and north."[18]

GOVERNMENT

A governor and his aides (a system instituted by the Spaniards) are elected annually in most of the villages. However, they have no real authority, but act merely as go-betweens for the priestly powers and the white man. The government is actually carried on through the ruling religious groups. In the west the Priest of the Zenith (or Sun), who inherits his office, stands at the head of the council and acts as leader. When the moiety divides the town into Summer and Winter people, there is a priest head and his council for each group, one serving throughout the first and the other throughout the second part of the yearly round.

MANNERS

The Pueblos are a modest people—polite, well behaved, and noted for mildness of manner. Ruth Benedict points out that "the southwest pueblos are . . . Apollonian, and in the consistency with which they pursue the proper valuations of the Apollonian they contrast with very nearly the

PLATE 3. *Saiyataca, Zuñi longhorn kachina mask. An excellent example of occult symmetry in design.*   ⟫→

Plate 3

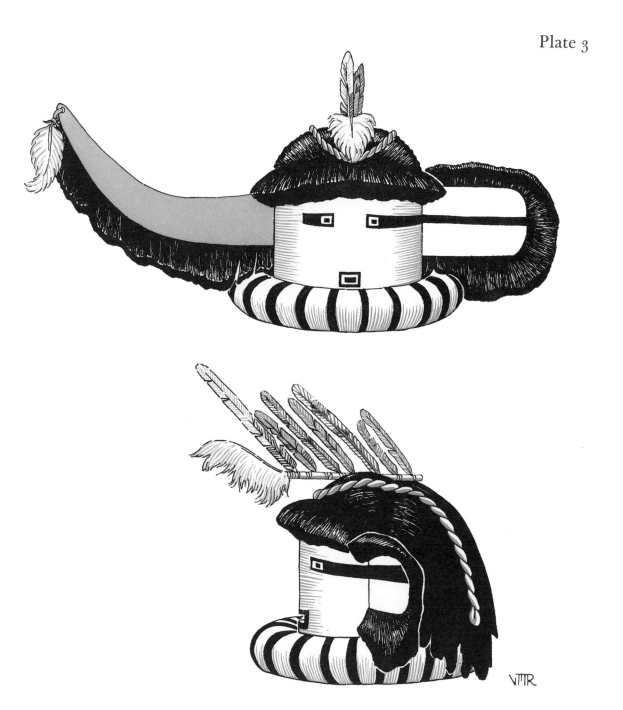

whole of aboriginal America; they possess in a small area islanded in the midst of predominantly Dionysian cultures an ethos distinguished by sobriety, by its distrust of excess, that minimizes to the last possible vanishing point any challenging or dangerous experiences. They have a religion of fertility without orgy. They have abjured torture. They indulge in no wholesale destruction of property at death. They have never made or bought intoxicating liquors in the fashion of other tribes about them, and they have never given themselves up to the use of drugs. They have even stripped sex of its mystic danger. They allow to the individual no disruptive role in their social order.''[19]

Accompanying this sobriety and evenness there is a pronounced secretiveness which makes it almost impossible to disentangle their extraordinarily complex religious and ceremonial life. For centuries they have successfully evaded the curious and the inquiring. Even the Catholic friars who came up from Mexico to establish religious centers and to 'convert the heathen' were able to scratch only the surface of their ceremonial system, and instead of bringing salvation to the 'heathen' they found in the end that there remained only the same Indian rite clothed superficially in Catholic custom. The saints' days are celebrated, to be sure, on dates stipulated by the Church, and these celebrations may include the usual Mass and church observances, followed by general festivity; but the dance, the native prayer and worship, the fundamental aspect of Pueblo religion is as Indian today as it was before Coronado's visit in 1540.

RELIGION

"The religious life of the Pueblos," says Edgar L. Hewett, "is the key to their existence. Their arts, industries, social structure, government, flow in orderly sequence from their beliefs concerning nature and deific power. . . . In its essence it is almost what modern science has attained to—the conception of Nature and God as one.''[20]

It is readily understood why the Indian felt so dependent upon the sky, the earth, the sun, and the natural elements. He needed all these for the cultivation of his crops, from which he provided himself with food and clothing, and these things were needed for the growth of game. Everything in his daily existence depends upon them. He considers himself at one with the things about him. The whole world seems animate: each object in space or time exists and has a personality. There is no more concern over personal religious experience than over personal prestige and profit. His own importance in the scheme of existence is no more than that of a tree or a rabbit. "The religion of the Pueblos . . . rests on two basic ideas: namely, a belief in the unity of life as manifested in all things, and in a dual principle in all existence, fundamentally, male and female."[21]

Pantheon of supernaturals.—To this unified belief in nature there is added the belief that certain attributes exist only in particular forces. From this springs a kind of pantheon of supernaturals who embody these forces. Varying little throughout, they may be classed as: cosmic—sun, moon, stars, earth, and wind; animal—beast of prey, water serpent, and spider; ancestral, or the dead in general—the kachina, the skeleton, and the war gods.[22] All these supernaturals exhibit anthropomorphic characteristics and are said in myth to have mingled among men in human form. "Even the spirits conceived of as animals have only to remove their skins and they will become men in shape and appearance, although retaining their supernatural attributes and powers."[23] These supernaturals are graded according to their power and are believed to live in the under regions of the world as well as the four quarters and the heavens above. The importance attributed to them in the different pueblos seems to vary as the sphere of influence or function which they represent is of importance to that group.

Organizations.—These forces, or beings, may be either friendly or hostile. They require respect and veneration. Gifts and assistance are sought from them by offerings, prayers, or magical practices, carried on by a complicated group of secret societies and fraternities.

These societies are practically unlimited and there is scarcely a limit to the number to which each man may belong. At adolescence every boy is initiated into a kachina cult or kiva society, an esoteric group which approaches the supernatural through ritual and sometimes through impersonation. A youth or man may, through a vow made in sickness, be promised to one of the medicine societies found throughout the pueblos, except in Picuris and Taos, where the kiva societies perform these rites; or, if he 'takes a scalp', he is forced to join the warriors' society to 'save' himself. He may be called upon to join the priesthood or, if he is connected with a sacerdotal household, he may be asked to fill an official position, or he may be appointed or elected to it. There are also innumerable cults. "Most men of advanced age are affiliated with several of these groups."[24]

Each esoteric cult is dedicated to the worship of some special supernatural or group of supernaturals. Each has a priesthood, a pattern of ritual, permanent paraphernalia, a calendric cycle of ceremonies, and a special place for the rehearsals, rites, and performances.

Kiva.—In each pueblo there are two or more kivas.[25] A kiva* is a chamber or room built especially for the meetings of a group and used by its members as a clubhouse for the men, where they come together to talk and work.[26] It is here that many of the semipublic ceremonies take place. At certain times it can be called the theater for religious entertainment.

At Hopi each village has six kivas, in accordance with the cardinal directions. These are subterranean rooms, sometimes built in the mesa side with one exposed wall in which a small hole admits light and air, the roof being kept level with the mesa top. The rooms are rectangular and measure about twenty-five feet long and some fifteen feet wide.[27] About one-third of the floor space is raised a foot above the rest. This may be reserved for spectators of the indoor performances. In the center of

---

* "Kiva," says Ruth Bunzel, "is a Hopi word which has become the standardized term . . . for the ceremonial rooms of peculiar construction which are found in all ancient and modern pueblos."

the roof is the entrance hatchway, through which the long ladder extends. Directly below this opening is the fireplace, a pit which uses the hatchway as a smoke hole. At the lower end a plank with a tightly plugged hole covers a cavity in the floor which represents the place of emergence from the inner worlds, and through which the prayers of the people are supposed to return to the Great Ones. Along one or more side walls is an earthen ledge which serves as a seat and, at the lower end, provides a shelf upon which religious paraphernalia are placed.

The six ceremonial chambers at Zuñi are square buildings incorporated in the house units. There is a hatchway entrance from above, as well as a communicating door to an adjoining house, and a small wall opening on the street side for air. A covered fireplace is found directly below the hatchway and earth ledges are built out from the walls. However, here there is no hole to the underworld.[28]

At Acoma, also, the seven ceremonial chambers are in the house blocks. They are designated as special buildings by the double ladders which lead to their roofs. The poles of these ladders are longer than ordinary, and the crosspieces at the tops are carved with designs suggestive of lightning symbols.[29] Only one of the Acoma chambers has the planked resonance hole in the floor.

One other kiva form is significant. In the Rio Grande region separate circular buildings may be found beside the dance plaza. They are semi-subterrane, and sometimes the tops are built to a considerable height. A fine example at San Ildefonso has an outside stairway leading to the top, where a ladder through a hatchway leads one down into the interior. A small opening on the side provides light and air. At one dance I saw there, the more slender and agile dancers climbed in and out through this opening. In some places these round houses appear to be used by different groups and constitute a dressing room or exhibit space for ceremonies;[30] other rooms or kivas in the various Rio Grande pueblos serve as society

PLATE 4. *Hehea, Hopi mask, with collar of evergreen.*   ⟫⟫→

Plate 4

and moiety headquarters. There may be several different types of kivas in one village; for example, Isleta has two round houses, two detached rectangular houses, and a separate building for general assemblage.[31]

Ritual.—"There are definite fixed rituals and prayers for every ceremonial occasion."[32] The general form is a retreat followed by a dance.

FIGURE 3. Round kiva at San Ildefonso.

The retreat is always private, but the dance may be performed publicly in the plaza or semiprivately in the kivas or houses of the cult groups or in the home of the leader.

Along the Rio Grande the retreat lasts from one to four nights; farther west the retreat and subsequent dances may require as many as sixteen days. It is often preceded by a public announcement from the chief or town crier. For the period of retreat an arrangement of sacred objects is made at one end of the kiva. A formal altar of painted wooden slats is erected and decorated with feathers and spruce boughs. On the floor in front of the altar is a painting of special significance. It is made by a priest, and his materials are colored sands or corn meal, which he allows to run through his fingers into compositions delicate and beautiful. Bowls of medicine water and various objects with fetishistic powers are handled and set upon stipulated spots about the altar. Perfect ears of corn, which sometimes are hollowed out and filled with a variety of native-grown seeds and decorated with beads and feathers, symbolize life tokens and represent the ceremonial chief, the clan head, or the individual society members. Crudely cut stone animal forms, wooden images, masks, and claws and skins of beasts of prey are placed in orderly groups. Altar masks are rarely worn in ceremonies. They are supposed to have come to the earth with the Pueblo people, and since they are so very old, they are regarded with great respect.[33]

Accompanying this altar setup are certain prayers and ritualistic observances. The most stylized as well as the most casual pattern is surrounded by a great background of myth and legend. These are handed down by word of mouth, and it is an important duty of men old in office and in years to instruct the younger men in all ritual forms, at the same time reminding the others of their backgrounds and origins. The form of the ritual is that of a chant which retells the myth centering in this particular rite and thus forms a background for the appearance of certain characters and the final public demonstration. Leslie White says of a religious observance at Santo Domingo: "The retreat as well as the subsequent masked dance is a little play. The medicine men go back to Shipap [the place of their emergence] to see the mother . . . to get her to send [the Cloud People]. Hence the chamber into which the society retires is called Shipap. For four days the medicine men are not seen at all, for they are not in the pueblo. They are in Shipap. After the retreat is over the doctors reappear . . . and a masked dance is held [they have brought the Shiwanna* back with them]."[34]

Those in retreat practice various forms of abstinence. Meat, grease, and salt are abstained from, and at certain times there is absolute fasting. Continence preceding and during any ceremonial action is held to be particularly important. Purification is required in all the pueblos. Bathing, especially washing of the hair, is of great significance. To insure in-

---

* Shiwanna means Rain Makers, anthropomorphic spirits who bring rain.

ternal purification, emetics are taken each morning of the retreat and after the final dance.

The men who take part in the retreat are virtually prisoners. They spend all their time in the kiva or society chamber, where they perform rituals or prepare offerings, costumes, and the paraphernalia for the final performance.

The most common offering is the prayer stick. Its appearance and manufacture will vary with the pueblo in which it is made and the supernatural to whom it is dedicated. It is usually a small stick carefully smoothed and painted, and it has a dressing of various feathers attached with a homespun cotton cord. These are placed before ancient shrines or buried in the fields or at the river's edge. Another form of offering is corn meal or pollen. This may be sprinkled on the dancers, the altars, and the paraphernalia. Every morning those who hold sacerdotal positions make offerings of corn meal to the Sun. Corn meal is significant in every altar ceremony.

Cults.—The Pueblo Indian early believed that he was dependent upon the Great Ones for his sustenance and well-being. Hence there grew up a cult, the Kachina Cult, for the worship of these Great Ones; and likewise cults of veneration for those beings or forces which regulated other phases of his existence. Inimical beings developed the War Cult; the desire for meat and skins created the Hunt groups; and the mysteries of bodily ills brought about the Medicine societies, the animal patrons of which were supposed to give them insight and power.

"The katcina cult is built upon worship principally through impersonation of a group of supernaturals."[35] Their cult "seems to be the most fundamental aspect of pueblo religion, although the katcina cult itself is probably a later overlay, upon an older weather control organization. The katcina spirits are supernaturals who bring rain and good health. They were created at the time of the first emergence of the people from their underground home or shortly thereafter. Some of the pueblos say that part of the people fell in the water and were drowned after the emergence, thus becoming katcina."[36]

These supernaturals live in an underground world[37] or beneath the surface of the Sacred Lake, as at Zuñi.[38] The new-born are thought to come from one of these places, and the dead return there. Here the kachinas spend their time in singing and dancing. They possess rich clothing, valuable beads, and beautiful feathers. A very long time ago, the legends tell, the kachinas, whenever the people were lonely and sad, would come to entertain them with singing and dancing in the plazas, or perhaps in specially prepared houses of the pueblo. This would bring gaiety and joy to all the people. When the fields were parched and dry, the kachinas would come bringing the refreshing and revivifying rain. They particularly watched over the Pueblo peoples and provided for them. At Zuñi, it is said that each time the kachinas came they took one of the people back with them into the underground world; thus at Zuñi the joy at the coming of the kachinas was not unmixed with sorrow.[39] At Acoma there was a great fight because the people had mocked and criticized the kachinas.[40] As a result the kachinas decided that it would be better if they no longer visited the village in person. They therefore showed the people how to copy their masks and costumes, taught them their songs and dances, and exhorted them to perform the dances correctly, to live good lives in observation of custom and ritual, and to honor and respect the kachina. In return the supernaturals would come and be with them in spirit and would bring prosperity.

As soon as the impersonator dons the mask of the supernatural, he is believed to become that spirit. As a consequence he is supernatural and must not be approached or touched during the ceremonies, and he must be discharmed after the ceremonies before he again becomes mortal. "Instituted according to tradition, solely as a means of enjoyment, they

PLATE 5. *Many-colored Zuñi Salimapiya of the Zenith, with collar of raven's feathers, bandoleer pouch, and special feather mask ornament.*   ⟫⟫→

Plate 5

[the kachina ceremonies] have become the most potent of rain-making rites, for since the divine ones no longer appear in flesh they come in their other bodies, that is, as rain."[41]

"The katcina or masked figure has been as baffling in pueblo ceremonialism as any of its baffling features. The general concept of the katcina is simple enough. A wearer of the mask represents, in fact embodies, a beneficent supernatural bringer of rain and of abundant crops, but in the katcina conceptual complex in detail there is considerable variation as to particular supernaturals, their origin and their habitats: and as for katcina ceremonial organization or rather association of the katcina with ceremonial organizations, that differs everywhere, from tribe to tribe, even from town to town."[42]

Throughout the span of pueblos all the men belong to one or more tribal units which are associated with the Kachina Cult. In a few villages where the cult is nonexistent the ceremonial organizations center in the moiety, replete with secret rites and ritualistic paraphernalia. In the western pueblos there are six kachina groups, identified with the six directions: south, west, east, north, zenith, and nadir. Each one is lodged in its own kiva. Women, girls, and uninitiated boys are supposed not to know that the supernaturals are being impersonated by their own clansmen.

The dance.—The climax of each ceremonial period is the prayer drama, a reverential, solemn, ecstatic final dance. It comes at the end of the rigors of retreat and abstinence and concludes the myths and legends the unfolding of which constitutes each ceremonial observance. Originated to give joy and pleasure to the supernaturals, it has been continued as an entertainment for them and as a means of instruction, diversion, and worship for every man, woman, and child in the community. An eminent ethnologist has pointed out that here is "the best round of theatrical entertainment enjoyed by any people in the world, for nearly every ceremony has its diverting side, for religion and drama are here united as in primitive times."[43]

Even the simplest dance has a variety of patterns, and the artistic costuming and stylized action keep the spectators enthralled. A performance may pantomime the story of a certain culture hero, or a legendary figure, or it may exhibit a pageant of numerous and varied characters. The mimetic Animal and Bird dances revert to a belief in an animate world where, in the long ago, man and beast lived together and understood each other. In order to pantomime the hunt, that time must be reinfused with life as when animals gave their lives willingly to aid their human brothers. At the more elaborate dances the clowns are always present. Each village has two groups of very powerful priests who masquerade as grotesque characters symbolic of their mythical origins. The clown-priest phase is universal among all the pueblos, but the grotesquerie varies.

The Mudhead is a well-known Hopi-Zuñi clown with a baglike mask (pl. 40). This mask and the body of the clown are painted earth color with clay from the Sacred Lake. The "Chiffoneti"* of the Rio Grande region are unmasked (pl. 39), and their bodies are painted in black and white stripes to represent the spirits of the dead. Although these clowns are the most powerful priests and intermediaries to the gods, they act the buffoon and perform impromptu interludes between the dances. They make sport of individual and group, caricaturing individual eccentricities or satirizing group foibles, and when a direct hit is scored the glee of the nonvictims breaks forth in raucous laughter. They are the censors, the mediators, and the judges for the social life of the village. Sometimes they play games or mimic the performance just ended.

These clowns are always present at kachina dances. Herbert Spinden repeats in part the dialogue with which they drew the Cloud People to a certain ceremony:

"At the appointed time all the villagers go to the underground lodge and seat themselves in readiness for the performance. Soon two clowns appear at the hatchway in the roof and come down the ladder. They

---

* A present-day Mexican term, commonly used.

make merry with the spectators. Then one says to the other: "My brother, from what lake shall we get our masked dancers tonight?' 'Oh, I don't know. Let's try Dawn Canyon Lake. Maybe some Cloud People are stopping there.' Then one clown takes some ashes from the fireplace and blows it out in front of him. 'Look, brother', he says, 'do you see any Cloud People?' They peer across the ash cloud and one says, 'Yes, here they come now. They are walking on the cloud. Now they stop at Cottonwood Leaf Lake.' Then the other clown blows ashes and the questions are repeated. Thus the Cloud People are drawn nearer and nearer until they enter the village. The clowns become more and more excited and finally cry, 'Here they are now!' and the masked dancers stamp on the roof and throw game, fruit and cakes down the hatchway.'"

Since the Pueblo Indians are fundamentally a peace-loving people, the so-called "war dances" were usually borrowed, sometimes actually purchased, from other tribes which were often their deadliest enemies. These dances then were known by that tribe's name, that is, Navaho, Pawnee, or Apache. The ceremony of the dance is learned in its entirety, even to the chant in a foreign language, and the dress is copied or simulated. Thus the dance can be used as counter-magic against those who originated it, although it is sometimes used merely as picturesque entertainment.

As we have noted, the dance is the event of principal importance in all these ceremonial performances. It is not a dance such as we are familiar with, but a stately movement to a solemn chant—a symbolic and pictorial rhythm which is an outgrowth of prayer just as were the medieval dramas when the Biblical stories were unfolded in action before the high altar. The result is prayer and entertainment, church and theater. Those who perform believe they are benefiting the entire community, even the outside world. Those who watch have also lent their support. During the days of retreat and ceremony the preparation of food for the performers falls upon the women members. Often one society will provide the dance which accompanies the prayers of another society performing the kiva rites. Each person in the village gives offerings and blessings. For the final performance the people stand silently in solid blocks, looking down from the terraced housetops, or they sit motionless upon the plaza ledges. Between dances there is quiet conversation, gossip, or the subdued hailing of visitors from a far-off pueblo. These are community affairs and everyone must take part at some time during the year. The Zuñi kiva societies are required to present at least three group dances from one winter solstice to the next.⁵ Thus those who do not perform are always interested and sympathetic spectators.

At the dances performed in the individual society rooms the audience is composed mainly of the women and children group members, as the men are usually participating. Seated along the sides of the room or at the raised end, they remain quietly attentive, without a change in expression, watching for hours the movement of the dance. Several groups may combine for a presentation in which each performs its own act or dance. These separate numbers are repeated simultaneously in each of the participating kivas.

The dance patterns are very simple. The most common is a long line which moves as a single unit. There may be one row of men working in perfect unison, one foot of each man raised to the same height at the same moment; or there may be two rows facing each other, with steps varied to suit the type of impersonation. Dancers depicting male characters dance more forcefully than those depicting female characters. In the Rain Dance the line of fifty or sixty dancers is squared around three sides of the plaza, but there is no circular action. The dancers themselves turn, and pause, and turn again, the sweep of movement running through the line like a breath of wind through stalks of ripening grain.

A circular pattern is followed in the women's society dances and in

PLATE 6. *Zuñi blue Salimapiya of the West, whose body stain is the fluid from corn-husks. A special kilt has a wide border of embroidery. Prophetic yucca leaves are carried.*   ⇛→

Plate 6

those performed for curing and for war. The movement is continuous in one direction, with the participants facing the center.

A more elaborate pattern is made up of several movements. In the Rio Grande pueblos, "the public dances in the plaza are more or less processional but the advance is very slow. There are definite spots of stationary dancing and here countermarching is used to make a new quadrille-like formation."[46] Two men are followed by two women, each pair dancing as a single unit. There are no complicated figures or interweaving of dancers.

The dance steps look extremely simple. The usual one consists of a vigorous stamping with the right foot while the heel of the left foot is only slightly raised. In more lively dances both feet leave the ground alternately and give the appearance of sustaining the body in air. About these steps there is a feeling of eternity, as if, since time began, generations, nay, races of dancers had beaten with their feet the surface of the earth to obtain from it strength and power. Women often dance barefoot in order to receive fecundity from the mother of mothers. There are few arm gestures and little posturing. Each dancer has splendid body control. It is enthralling to see the vigorous movement continue without a break for fifteen or twenty minutes at regular intervals throughout the day.

Certain of the Bird dances require great strength and skill for the wheeling and circling movements which give the illusion of winged flight. The footwork is sure and delicate and the precision of each performance is remarkable. These dances as a whole are full of color and imaginative stylization based upon a hypnotic rhythm. The peculiar pulsation is almost impossible to imitate for anyone not born to the sound. The rhythm is regular, but there are skip beats and pauses which occur simultaneously in drumbeat, song, and dance.

Usually, percussion instruments provide the accompaniment for the dance. Drums vary from hollowed logs and pottery jars with skin heads to flat tom-toms. They are beaten with sticks made with a hooped end or wrapped with cotton. Rattles of gourd, turtle shell, and rawhide bags filled with pebbles or seeds are carried by most of the dancers.⁴⁷ Notched sticks may be rasped against each other on a sounding board of wood or gourd. Occasionally, bird-bone whistles are heard—shrill notes above the steady drone of drumbeat and human voice.

All dances are also accompanied by songs or chants sung by a chorus or by the dancers themselves. Some of the songs are so old that the lan-

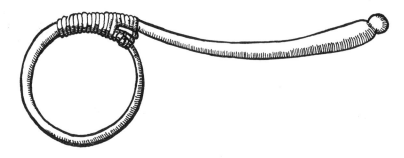

FIGURE 4. Hopi drumstick, bent into shape when green and bound with deerskin thong, forming a looped end.

guage is obsolete and even the singers do not know the meanings of the sounds. On the other hand, some of the old dances have new songs composed for them for each performance.⁴⁸

The masked dances, even those in which female characters appear, are performed exclusively by men. Women take part in most of the other dances. The Corn Dance has an equal number of men and women. The Hunt Pantomimes have one or two maidens who personify the animal mothers. The women's societies perform dances in which only women and girls take part.

The dance leader always takes his position in the center of the line. The priest of the group appears at the head of the line. He does not dance, but stands chanting or praying as he displays a feather badge of office or a banner of ceremonial significance. Whenever a chorus is required, it is grouped around him.

CEREMONIAL CALENDAR

Every pueblo determines its own special calendar of ceremonies by observation of the sun. Some authorities think that the Rio Grande pueblos have adopted the white man's calendric system, thereby changing the yearly pattern. This seems to be borne out in the election of governors and the saint's day festivals, but the dances with seasonal significance are still performed in proper relation to the native calendric periods. The summer solstice and the winter solstice were the two divisions of the ceremonial year. The Indian "observed that the sun, both to the east and to the west, reached a point in the south beyond which it never traveled, and from which it commenced its return to the north. In due time the return of the sun dispelled the cold of the winter and brought warmth and life back to the earth."[49]

Thus the rituals and ceremonies closely follow the seasons. In spring, the rituals of the planting are followed by the ceremonies for germination and growth. In summer, the rites of protection of the crops coincide with the ceremonies to invoke rain. The autumn is filled with dances of thanksgiving as the gathering of the harvest evokes prayers for the fertility of the earth for the coming year. The winter season is filled with invocations. Many of these are made by the Weather Control groups, who must provide snow in the mountains to fill the rivers in spring, and at the same time man and animal must be protected from fierce blizzards and freezing winds. Many prayer ceremonies are performed by the Hunt groups, which are active at this time. The prayers and dances are a form of appeal to the animals. Formerly this appeal was that they allow themselves to be killed for the benefit of mankind; now, since there is government restriction on hunting, the appeal is that the animals intercede with the 'higher powers' to provide for man.

Thus there is an ever-recurring cycle of events to assure the continuation of life by providing food, clothing, and health.[50]

THE INFLUENCE OF THE CATHOLIC CHURCH

The Catholic Church has had an important influence on the lives of the Pueblo Indians, because of the missions which were established along the Rio Grande. Early in the seventeenth century, Franciscan missionaries were sent to all the villages in an attempt to convert the inhabitants to the Christian faith. A very few accepted it to the exclusion of their own beliefs. With the characteristic openmindedness of their race they have assumed the outward manifestation of a belief in God, but only as He is related to their pantheon of deific powers. An attempt was made to prohibit their native ceremonies as inimical to Christian beliefs. The Church objected to the worship of their supernaturals, and as a result kachina rituals were performed in secret, excluding all who were not initiated into the Indians' beliefs and customs.[51] Even today, when these rites are being celebrated, all unbelievers are requested to leave the village, and the streets are patrolled to guard against the intrusion of any outsiders.

The practice of exclusion has made it well-nigh impossible for any knowledge of the secret ceremonies to be obtained. Among the Hopi, where Spanish occupation was brief, there is no exclusion from rites which are public to the natives. Certain kiva ceremonies, however, are always secret and are known only to the initiated. At Zuñi, where Spanish occupation ended less than a century ago, Americans are admitted to all ceremonies, but Mexicans are excluded. It is from Hopi and Zuñi that the most information can be obtained concerning the sacred supernaturals who are featured in their masked dances.[52]

When the priests of the Rio Grande missions saw that their attempts to check the native ceremonialism were vain, they encouraged certain acts of ritual, other than those pertaining to the kachinas, as an added feature of their church days. Thus today we find many of the dances appearing hand in hand with the Catholic service. To each village a patron saint was allotted. On the church day set aside for the veneration of this saint there has been instituted a particular celebration combining both the Catholic and the native ceremonies; for instance, the celebration of St. Stephen's Day at Acoma.

Early on the morning of September 2, St. Stephen's Day, the visiting priest may be seen climbing the rugged mesa trail. He performs Mass in the old adobe mission, built in 1699 by the hard labor of the natives subjugated under the tyrannical power of the resident priest. The devout come to the church and pray. Marriages are performed and babies are baptized. Then, with lighted candles, the statue of their saint carried bravely beneath a garish canopy, they march in solemn procession around the terraced house blocks of their pueblo to the beat of an Indian drum and the wail of a pagan chant. At length, when the sacred image is couched in a temporary bower of tall cornstalks and evergreens, the typical Indian dance is performed in its honor. Turning before the holy figure, they beat and pound the earth with their feet, singing to other gods their songs of prayer and thanksgiving.

Several religious playlets have been devised from sixteenth-century ecclesiastical drama, but these are costumed in accordance with modern Indian ingenuity and provide nothing of interest in the way of native ceremonial dress.

Indian life is at present taking on new proportions; the American schools are effecting a change in standards, and native ceremonial forms will probably not continue throughout another generation. Not many years hence we shall see the trappings of that religious and artistic climax of the Pueblo Indian's life consigned to stuffy museums and to long, dryly informative reports by eminent ethnologists.

PART TWO

Costume Materials and Their Significance

ALL THE IMPORTANT ceremonies in the life of man are accompanied by manifestations in connection with dress. One of the fundamental characteristics of the human race is the desire to be dressed appropriately for an occasion. Man sets aside special ornamentation for his prayer and his drama. In order to appreciate his ceremonial costumes it is necessary to have a knowledge of his life and his habits.

The materials from which costumes are made vary with the geographical conditions under which a people live and with the degree of that people's cultural development. Among the Pueblos, articles of dress and ornament are the evolution of long experimentation in the manipulation of objects offered to them by nature, together with those which have been acquired through cultivation, invention, and trade.

FABRICATION OF CLOTH

If the finished garment is to be appreciated fully, it is necessary to understand the method of fabrication which has made it possible, because its final appearance is based upon this and upon the materials used. We must remember that cloth fabric is a result of a series of operations which convert a mass of loose fibers into a woven material. The kind of fiber and the manner in which it is treated distinguish one cloth from another. Thus a cotton yarn and a woolen yarn of the same weight, though woven in a similar manner, do not result in fabrics which feel or hang alike. On

[47]

the other hand, the same cotton yarn may be woven by two different processes and produce fabrics which vary in body and surface texture.

Weaving done by hand is a result of plaiting or braiding three or more strands of material. This is the most primitive method, but alongside of it we find the free use of mechanical devices such as the loom.

"In the Southwest, braiding was known to the earliest people of whom we have gained sufficient knowledge to venture upon giving them a name—the Basketmakers. It therefore has some two thousand years of antiquity in this instance, for these people were flourishing and making attractive braided sashes . . . as early as the time of Christ." These can be traced through prehistoric Pueblo periods down to the present day in the plaited white cotton ceremonial sash so commonly used.

One other form of yarn manipulation is that of looping, a process which we recognize as knitting or crocheting. It depends upon a continuous series of interlocking loops which do not require a foundation and which proceed in a transverse direction with a single strand of yarn. Originally a finger process, it soon developed simple tools—the needles for knitting and the hook for crocheting. The development of these instruments marked a decided advance in technique. "Ancient peoples used needles of wood or bone"[2] to fashion garments from vegetable fibers and hair as well as from cotton and wool. Today the best examples of this art are the crocheted or knitted legging and footless stocking and the crocheted shirt. Although it is likely that these garments were introduced by the Spaniards, it seems probable that the looping process itself is older.

Fiber.—Many different materials have been used in the process of weaving. Milkweed fiber has been employed, as well as small quantities of the hair of dog, mountain sheep, and bear, and even that of human beings.[3] Early in the Basketmaker era it was discovered that a fiber could

---

PLATE 7. *Zuñi Shalako, one of six giant messengers of the gods. This ten-foot effigy is balanced on a pole above the impersonator, who peeps through an opening between the top of the ceremonial blanket, used as a skirt, and the folds of the overlapping mantle.* ⋙→

Plate 7

be produced from the yucca plant. This "yucca fiber, alone or in combination with cotton, was of great importance as a weaving material. The
fur of beaver, otter, or rabbit was incorporated with yucca cord or twisted
around it to make warmer or more ornamental fabrics."[4] Even today the
leaves of the yucca are softened by boiling with cedar ash, and when cool
are drawn between the teeth in order to separate and cleanse the fibers.
When soaking makes them pliable for use, they are rolled into rope or
spun into a stiff thread for weaving.[5] Prehistoric remains have yielded
us examples of bags, sandals, sashes, crude kilts, and clouts thus fashioned.
Cedar bark was shredded and plaited and doubtless served the same purpose. Rabbitskins were cut while green into thin strips, and after drying
and curing were woven into blankets and mats.

Materials so produced, however, were rough and clumsy: it was the
use of cotton which introduced cloth and garments of an advanced kind.
"Throughout the first four Pueblo periods cotton was the staple product
from which cloth fabrics were made."[6] Cotton cloth has been unearthed
in prehistoric ruins and burial places.* Cotton was grown wherever it
could be cultivated, over almost the entire Southwest from the San Juan
River on the north as far west as the Colorado and along the Rio Grande to
the east.[7] In 1540 Coronado and his followers recorded its growth among
the Tewa and its use at Zuñi.[8] By 1582 we learn from Espejo and Luzán[9]
that it was in use among the Hopi, where, if we may judge by the great
number and the beauty of the blankets displayed to them, weaving from
cotton was undoubtedly a craft of long standing and high development.

About this time, also, feather mantles were in use. They were made
by tying long eagle feathers in horizontal rows to a cotton base, in the
process of weaving (pl. 2). The downy feathers of the eagle, the duck,
and the turkey were twisted into the yarn in the process of spinning and
this resulted in a cloth with a furry surface.[10]

---

* For example, on a body found in Cañada del Muerto, Arizona. The inner wrapping consists of
two white cotton blankets, outside of which is a fine feather blanket bound by hanks of cotton yarn.
Burial date, *ca.* 1000 A.D. Exhibit, Museum of Natural History, New York.

The Spaniards introduced sheep among the Pueblos, and thenceforth throughout their historic period woolen yarn and cloth played an important part; for all practical purposes woolen cloth replaced the former skin garments and the feather and cotton textiles. Cotton, however, has always been retained as a special ceremonial material, and it was always an article of luxury because of the small quantity which could be gathered within a single year and the tedious labor required to prepare it for use. Although it is not now grown, raw cotton and cotton batting are still sold to the Indians to be spun by hand into thread and woven by hand into cloth for certain sacred garments.

We are mainly concerned with the two fabrics, cotton and wool, which make up the principal woven articles of clothing.

Formerly this cotton (technically known as *Gossypium Hopi* Lewton), grew wild,[11] a small boll with a tawny fiber. Later it was cultivated.[12] "The cotton seed was planted in holes about one and a half inches deep and covered with white sand. The garden patches were divided into sections about a foot and a half square by little dirt borders to make watering easier."[13] The bolls were picked, broken open, and the fiber sorted, cleaned, and straightened by hand. This cotton was a distinct species with plants presenting ripened bolls within eighty-four days from the time the seeds were planted.[14]

Wool, after it was cut from the sheep, went through the same hand process of sorting, cleaning, and straightening, although it was often washed with suds made from the yucca root to remove all dirt and animal grease. With the coming of civilization the commercial wool card, a combing and straightening instrument, was introduced. This prepared the fibers of both cotton and wool[15] for spinning.

Spinning.—The process of spinning produces a thread capable of being woven. The native spindle has a cylindrical wooden shaft about twenty inches long with one end rather sharply pointed. A whorl, or circular disk, of stone, bone, or wood is slipped over this shaft midway between the center and the butt end. This acts as a flywheel and also serves to keep the yarn on the shaft. The spinner "takes one end of the roll of combed fleece in the left hand and holds it against the point of the spindle, rapidly revolved by the right hand, until it catches and twists spirally down the spindle shaft, the butt of which rests on the ground. As the loose roll twists around the spindle it reduces rapidly in size. The reduction is increased by drawing the thread away from the spindle with fairly

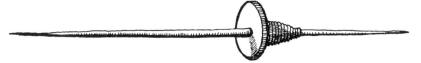

FIGURE 5. Spindle, with yarn below disk. The disk is made of horn, bone, stone, or wood, with a shaft of wood.

hard jerks. When a section has been brought to a quite small diameter it is allowed to roll up on the spindle shaft, after which a fresh arm's length is drawn out for spinning. When the spindle is full the yarn is removed and rolled into a ball. . . .

"The yarn produced by the first spinning is very coarse, lumpy and uneven, so that it has to be respun a number of times before it is fit for weaving. The finest and hardest yarn, used for warp, must be spun as many as six times."[16]

Good, hand-spun cotton produces a beautiful, coarse, irregular, creamy yarn. The woolen yarn is soft and lumpy. The differences in these yarns produce corresponding differences in the appearance and texture of the woven fabrics.

Weaving.—Weaving is done on a hand loom of the two-barred type, which is set up in the kiva or in the house. In all probability this loom originated either in Peru or in Middle America,[17] and thence was introduced among the early Pueblos. It is always associated with cotton, and cotton is associated with corn in the most generally accepted theory of the New World origins of agriculture.

To prepare the warp a frame is made, consisting of two square side bars and two round end bars. The yarn is tied to one end bar, then strung from the ball in a series of figure 8's over the end bars until the required width of warp is obtained. These loops are called sheds. The side bars are then removed and the end bars replaced by loom strings, which are fastened to the loom poles by heavy cords wrapped spirally between the warps. A simple support is made by fastening a crossbar to the roof beam or to hooks in the wall. From this hangs the yarn beam, a small pole held in place by a rope wound spirally around the two. The tension of the warp can be adjusted by tightening or loosening this rope. The upper loom pole is now swung from the yarn beam by a series of loops, and the lower pole is fastened at the bottom to another beam, which in turn is secured to pegs in the floor or specially made sockets.

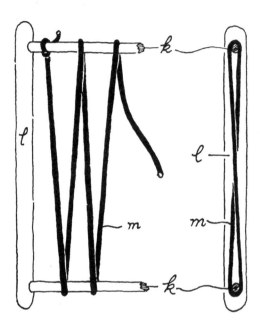

FIGURE 6. Warp setup on end bars. Side bar *l* holds end bars *k* in position so that warp *m* can be wrapped around them in figure-eight loops. The first sketch, front view; second, side view.

For weaving, a shed rod is placed in the upper loop to retain the original order and to separate the lines of warp. Loosely tied to the front threads of the lower shed is a heddle rod, by which the alternate series of warp threads can be drawn forward, allowing a passageway for the shuttle or bobbin carrying the weft or filler which completes the fabric web. This passage is further opened by the use of a batten, a smooth,

PLATE 8. *Special two-piece dance moccasin. Heelpieces are wound with white porcupine quills and black horsehair.*   ⋙→

Plate 8

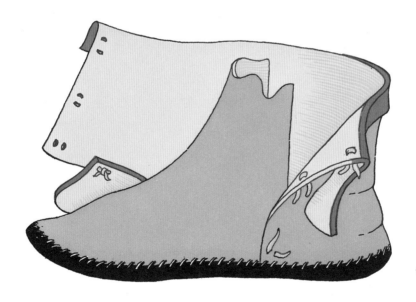

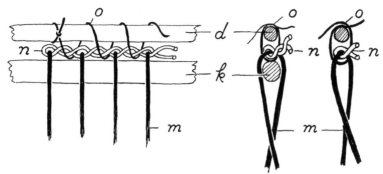

FIGURE 7. End bars replaced by loom strings. Heavy cord *n* is twisted between the warps *m*. Loom poles are tied to this twisted cord by twine *o*. The end bars *k* are then removed.

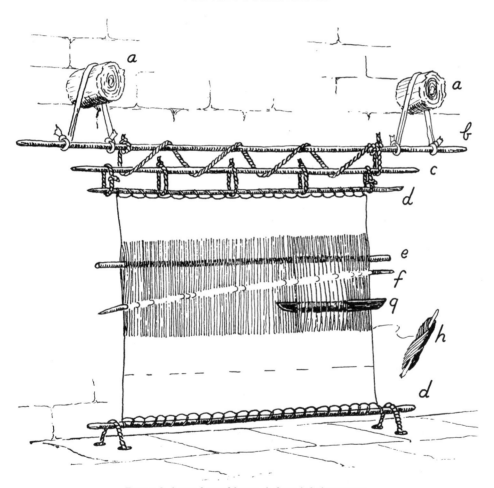

FIGURE 8. A two-barred loom. A dress is being woven.

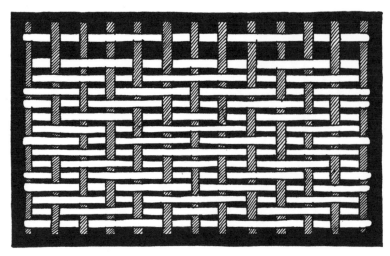

FIGURE 9. Diamond twill.

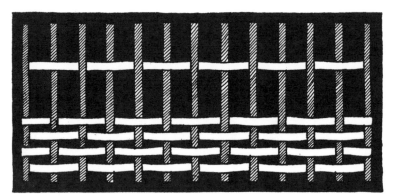

FIGURE 10. Plain weave.

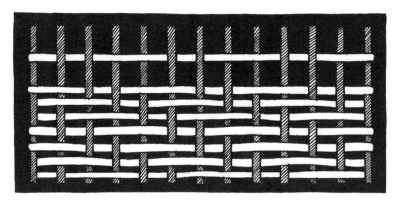

FIGURE 11. Diagonal twill.

thin board with beveled edges, which is threaded between the warp and by a dexterous twist holds the shed open by its width. The weft is then beaten down with the same tool.[18] Self patterns and surface textures result from use of the different weaves and depend upon various heddle setups. A plain weave is the simplest and undoubtedly was the first ever to be

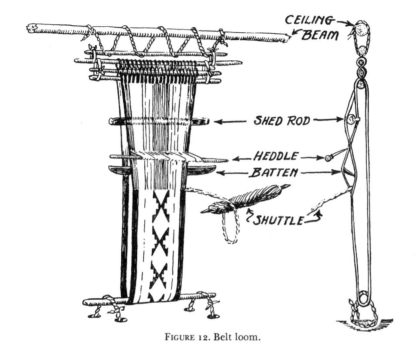

FIGURE 12. Belt loom.

adapted to a loom. A simple 'over one, under one' formula produces a fabric in which each thread of weft intersects that of the warp on the same vertical line and both are equally visible.

A similar setup in which the weft becomes the dominant element and is pressed down so tightly that the warp is hidden is called a tapestry weave. This produces a firm, stiff fabric. Designs are effectively made by varying the number of warp threads behind which the weft is allowed to pass, a method called warp floating. This is done with the fingers, without the use of a heddle device. The designs are always limited by straight lines, which tend toward a constant repetition of a unit figure.

Pueblo examples of this technique are the belts, sashes, and garters. For these a smaller loom is required, which also differs slightly from that used for large fabrics. It is called a belt loom.[19]

A twilled basket weave is produced when each line of weft intersects the warp at constantly varying points, or when the regular alternation of the point of intersection produces ribs which trend diagonally across the face of the fabric. The width of the stitch may vary; but at least every other stitch must be two or more warp strands in breadth in order to provide for the alternation of the intersections in regular order. This makes the twill.[20] Two variations of this method are to be observed: a diamond twill, in the border of women's dresses, and the diagonal twill, often seen in maidens' shawls.

A brocade weave is used to decorate the ends of a special sash for men. This is made by the Hopi. The result simulates embroidery, but the method is weaving. It consists of a secondary or overlaid weft which is woven through the warp independent of the original weft. Color is introduced in this second thread, and by picking out certain warp threads with the fingers or by substituting another color simple designs are made. These are restricted, however, by the right-angled intersections of the loom setup.[21]

The Hopi of today is the Pueblo 'textile manufacturer'. He is the master craftsman and trader. From his villages on the three mesas overlooking the Painted Desert he carries on an extensive trade with the Zuñi and the Rio Grande Pueblos, who depend upon him almost entirely for their native textiles. In exchange for their turquoises, shell necklaces, and money he gives them dresses, robes, kilts, and belts, which they in turn "embellish with embroideries to their individual liking."

There is evidence that weaving was done in other pueblos. The Zuñi still produce some dresses, belts, and blankets.[22] It is known that loom weaving was practiced by the Acoma, the Santa Clara, the Nambé, and

PLATE 9. *Squash-blossom ornament used on headdresses and masks.*   》》》→

Plate 9

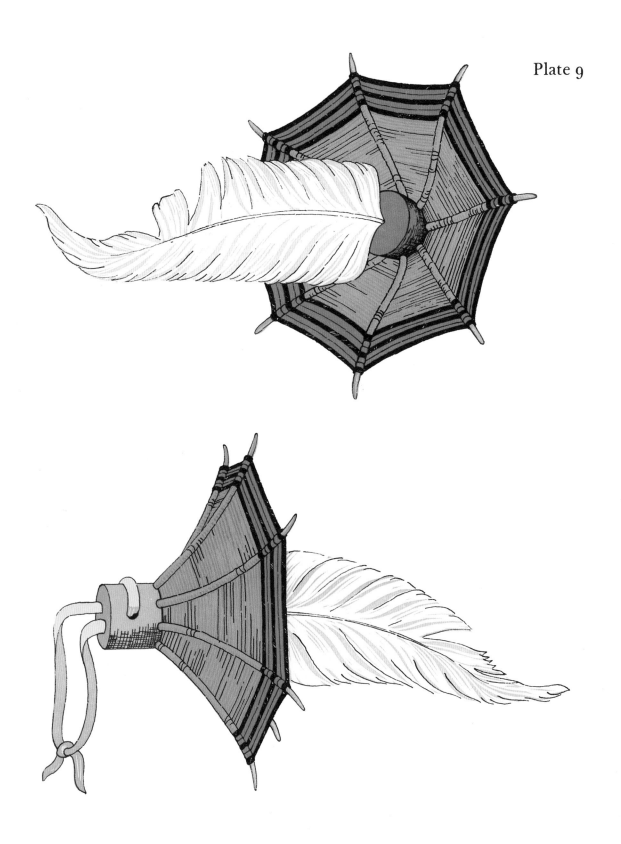

the Cochiti. However, these all depend upon Hopiland for those sacred garments which they carefully preserve for use on days of ceremony and entertainment.[23]

With very few exceptions men are the weavers* among the Pueblos.[24] They also make moccasins and the turquoise and silver jewelry, while the women make the pottery and weave the baskets.

PREPARATION OF SKINS

Tanned skins were useful for daily wear, and they supplemented cotton cloth, which, because of the time and labor required for its fabrication, could not have been produced in sufficient quantities. In the earliest Spanish records a follower of Coronado says of Zuñi: "The clothing of the Indians is of deerskin, very carefully tanned, and they also prepare some tanned cowhides [buffalo] with which they cover themselves, which are like shawls, and a great protection."[25]

The skins of wild animals are tanned and cured to make various garments and articles of ceremonial paraphernalia among the Pueblos. The material culture and the development of certain peoples are greatly influenced by the animals found in their districts. "The flesh . . . furnishes food, the skins provide raiment, thongs and other useful products, and bones furnish awls and other implements; but perhaps even more important from the cultural point of view, is the fact that animals enter largely into the mythology and religion."[26]

We find not only the names of clans and individuals emerging from this association, but special parts of animals becoming symbolic in religious observances, such as the use of bears' paws in the rite of curing and the use of the headdress of the buffalo skin and horns in the Animal Dance. Animal horns were used on other headdresses and masks. Rattles were made of bones and hoofs. Horsehair, goat and bear skins, and wool were sometimes dyed and used as beards, wigs, and ceremonial trimmings.

---

* The rabbitskin blankets were always woven by the women.

Even the six directions bore the symbols of various animals. Thus the mountain lion represented the north; the bear, the west; the badger, the south; the wolf, the east; the shrew, the nadir; and the zenith was represented by the eagle.

Furthermore, special qualities in certain leathers have produced a type of ceremonial apparel which could not have been realized had any other medium been employed. Helmet masks are fashioned from the heavy neckpieces of deerskin, buffalo hide, or present-day cowhide, while soft-tanned deerskin is made into kilts and mantles.

The variety of animals living on the arid plateaus of the Southwest was limited. The most familiar were probably antelope, coyote, and rabbit. Many legends center around the coyote, whose skin, it was believed, often concealed the metamorphosed body of some immortal creature. Rabbits were easily killed, and, since they were a prerequisite of the feast following the period of fasting and denial, they were hunted by large ceremonial groups, who encircled an allotted area, closed in on their prey and killed them with a throwing stick, a kind of boomerang which though curved did not return to its thrower.

Deer must have been plentiful, particularly in the winter when heavy snows in their high shelters forced them into the valleys in search of food.

Their beasts of prey were the bear, wildcat, mountain lion,[27] and fox. Of these the bear and the mountain lion were thought to be human beings who put on these skins at pleasure.[28] Great-horned mountain sheep were found in the high country on the south as well as in the Rocky Mountains on the north.[29] Likewise we are told of skunk,[30] squirrel,[31] porcupine, raccoon, badger, and otter. The former governor of Santa Clara wore summer ermine wrapped around his two braids when I called upon him at his home in the summer of 1936.

Through trade with other peoples the Pueblos were able to increase the quantity and variety of the skins which they used for their ceremonial and dress occasions.

Their neighbors to the east were Plains tribes whose existence centered in the herds of bison which roamed the prairie because it was mainly from these that they fed and clothed themselves. The need of a more varied diet sent these braves, who on other occasions were warlike, to barter their beautifully tanned leathers and pelts, preserved skulls, and bone beads for the delicious corn meal so painstakingly ground by the Pueblo women.[32] On the west, other seminomadic groups exchanged hides and pelts for the finely woven blankets, robes, and kilts of Hopi manufacture.[33]

As the Pueblos were a village people primarily concerned with agriculture, they depended for their food and clothing upon such crops as they could raise. They hunted only occasionally, in order to obtain skins for ceremonial needs and to procure the small amount of meat they needed to strengthen their vegetable diet. The hunt was a requirement prescribed by the War fraternity and directed by the warrior priests. To the Pueblo people all animals are living spirits and their right to exist is unquestioned. It is necessary, therefore, to pray to the animal and its family that it allow itself to be used for food and ceremony. After the kill, more rites must be observed, so that the spirit may not be displeased but may return to the other world and tell its kindred of the fine treatment accorded it.

The people of Taos and Picuris were descended from a Pueblo group who were tainted with the hunter's blood of the Apache and the Comanche. Living in close proximity to the plains, they had intermarried with the Plains Indians and had acquired habits resembling those of the aggressive, warlike marauders. They made long pilgrimages into the prairie country in search of bison.

Because they lived in the midst of wooded mountains, great herds of deer and elk came to the edge of their villages. It is not strange, therefore, that we find them much more influenced by their Plains brothers and eager to acquire the deerskin shirt and leggings, while their wives and daughters, Pueblo in their daily lives, sought to borrow the fringed dresses for their festival occasions. Here, then, we find a fusion of two cultures in dress and in society and ceremony. In contrast, along the Rio Grande, at Zuñi, and among the Hopi were people, peaceful by nature, who bartered their corn and turquoises for skins which they made up after their own traditional patterns.

Since the surrounding tribes clothed themselves in skins and their methods of tanning were practically the same, the Pueblo men undoubtedly knew the technique of skin dressing and employed it in much the same manner as their neighbors.

Certain steps had to be followed in skinning an animal. There must be no waste. All the hide was retained. Sometimes the paws and hoofs were kept intact. This principle can be observed in the pendent foxskins worn at Zuñi or the head preserved on the fawnskin bag worn over the shoulder of the Zuñi fire god.[34]

A concise description of the manner in which skins were dressed by the Plains Indians is given by Frederic Douglas: "First the wet hide was staked out on the ground, hair side down, and the flesh, fat, coagulated blood, and fragments of tissue scraped off with a toothed gouge or fleshing tool of bone or iron. Second, the hair was removed and the skin reduced to a uniform thickness by scraping, each side being worked over in turn with an adze-like tool."[35]

The immersion for a few days in a lye bath of ashes and water to aid in the removal of the hair[36] is suggested by Catlin.

"If rawhide was desired, nothing further was done to the hide. If soft flexible skin was needed, a third step was taken. A mixture of brains and any one or several of the following materials, cooked ground-up liver, fats and greases of various kinds, meat broth and various vegetable products, was thoroughly rubbed into the hide. When well saturated with this compound, it was allowed to dry, then soaked in warm water and

PLATE 10. *Tablet headdress worn by the Zuñi Corn Maidens. The natural hair shields the face.* (After Stevenson, 1904, pl. 37.)　　≫→

Plate 10

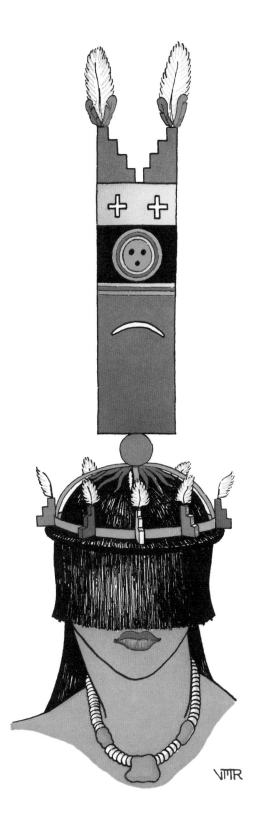

rolled up into a tight bundle. The final step was the stretching of the hide as the braining process caused great shrinkage. The hide was alternately soaked in warm water and pulled with hands and feet, pulled down over a rounded post, or stretched by two persons if the hide was large. Friction caused by rapidly pulling through a small opening was also resorted to to give greater softness. The dressing process was complete when the hide was nearly its original size and thoroughly softened and smoothed."[37]

Catlin describes a further step, that of smoking, which, he says, makes it possible for the skins, "after being ever so many times wet, to dry soft and pliant as they were before."[38]

It is true that the Indian dressed skin can be wet again and again and it will always dry with its original flexibility. This fact is made use of in the making of any special leather articles, such as moccasins and masks. The moccasin is cut to the pattern of the foot it is to cover, sewn, and packed in wet sand until saturated. The owner then allows it to dry on his foot, and shrinkage makes it fit perfectly.

The Havasupai, a group of seminomadic Indians who live in summer near their cornfields in Cataract Canyon—a deep chasm cutting into the south side of the Grand Canyon about a hundred miles west of the Hopi,—are also skillful tanners. They use a "process of rubbing beef brains and marrow and yucca pulp into the hides with the hands."[39] Many raw deer hides come to them from the Colorado River tribes farther to the west. These they tan and use in trade with the Hopi.

Among the Pueblos the tanning was done by the men; among the Plains tribes, by the women.

Pelts were cured in the same manner, but the hair was left on. The pelts, like the dressed skins, are impervious to water. A trader at Zuñi told me that the foxskin tailpieces (pl. 24) used in ceremonial dances were buried in damp sand for several days before being worn. They appeared, when brought out for wear, soft, sleek, and glossy.

FEATHERS

Throughout Indian lore, birds and feathers are prominent in myth and legend, in ceremony and drama. They are used as symbols in the religious and theatrical paraphernalia of the groups. In earlier days, they provided wearing apparel and were used lavishly in decoration. The Indian, living with few artificial aids, must depend upon nature and his own ingenuity to provide the decorative element.[40]

Birds were believed to possess the universal 'spiritual essences', and hence were rarely killed except as they were needed for food or as a measure to protect the newly sown corn. When feathers were needed for ornamentation, birds were plucked and their denuded bodies were encouraged, with artificial aids, to grow a new covering. The Zuñi plucking rites explain that the eagle's body is to be rubbed with kaolin, a white clay, and chewed corn so that more feathers will grow; the second growth will be very white.[41]

Of the many species of birds which inhabit these mesas and desert regions, certain ones have been predominantly associated with certain clans or moiety groups, or in some way connected with tribal divisions. Eagle, parrot, turkey, wild duck, goose, sandhill crane, crow, chaparral cock, dove, whippoorwill, golden warbler, magpie, hummingbird, and swallow are the names of clans, past and present, which have existed in some of the villages.[42] Such nomenclature appears to be only a name association, although there may be some totemic significance.

Some birds are associated with directions because of the color of their feathers. A prayer plume described by Stevenson allocates the long-tailed chat to the north, the long-crested jay to the west, the macaw to the south, the spurred towhee to the east, the purple martin to the zenith, and the painted bunting to the nadir.[43]

There are bird supernaturals which are impersonated in more or less stylized costumes. Among these are the eagle (pl. 24), red hawk, cock, turkey, wild duck, kite, crow, quail, mockingbird, and hummingbird.[44] Eastern Pueblo Bird Dances include the eagle (pl. 23), the crow, and the snowbird. These latter dances were done without masks, character illusion being given through costume and action.

Macaw.—Certain feathers were desired because of their colors (pl. 3). Those of the macaw were most highly valued, and they were also very difficult to procure. "Its feathers are highly prized by the Tewa for ceremonial purposes. They state that the feathers and also live . . . [birds] were obtained from Mexico in former times."[45] Runners were sent to the south to bring back many brilliantly colored feathers (pl. 3) of this prized bird in exchange for skins and turquoises. The kachinas are said to "wear macaw feathers because the macaw lives in the south and they want the macaw to bring the rain from the south. They always like to feel the south wind because the south wind brings rain."[46] There were many local birds the feathers of which were highly valued for various reasons: goose, wild duck, owl, jay, oriole, yellow warbler, goldfinch, one or more species of small red birds,[47] and the hummingbird.[48]

Turkey.—The turkey was domesticated at an early date. The Spaniards found many of these "cocks with great hanging chins,"[49] which roamed the country or were kept in large flocks chiefly to supply feathers for garments.[50] Turkey feathers are of some importance in ceremonial life. This is illustrated by a certain rite at Isleta, where the turkey feather as the "oldest one"[51] has a place of preëminence, being set aside for the chief. Since the turkey is hard to raise, there is a belief at Zuñi that its feathers are a token of mortality and that no dancer should wear them except one who impersonates supernaturals or the dead.[52] At Cochiti turkey feathers are buried on All Souls' Day so that the dead may wear them in their dances.[53]

Eagle.—"The eagle is symbolic of the sun or sky god."[54] His feathers, together with those of the turkey, are the most widely used. He is the messenger to the supernaturals and soars above the clouds to take prayers from earth creatures to the Great Ones. The eagle always represents the direction of the zenith, or above; he is the only bird used to indicate the ethereal heights. As we learn from the eagle myth: "The katcinas . . . wear these feathers because the eagle is strong and wise and kind. He travels far in all directions and so he will surely bring rain. The eagle feathers must always come first."[55] Both the long, stiff, tail and wing feathers and the downy white breast feathers (pl. 5) are important. The downy feathers belong to the Sun priest;[56] others may use them when rain is very much needed. In this connection they are primarily worn by the kachinas. In certain curing rites the doctors take 'sorceries' from the body of the patient. They hold eagle tail feathers in each hand and by brushing the patient and striking the feathers in one hand against those in the other they throw the evil in each direction: north, south, east, west, zenith, and nadir.[57] Eagle feathers generally enclose the sacred ear of corn; and they are used for leading persons to ceremonial places, for making certain ceremonial gestures, and for dipping medicines or sacred water from ceremonial bowls.[58]

In the Snake Dance of the Hopi, one of the dancers follows the snake carrier and continually brushes the waving rattler with an eagle-feather wand in order to prevent him from striking. The gatherer, or guard, who picks up the wriggling snakes after their dance turn and before they can escape, controls them with eagle plumes. The brushing movement along its back prevents the snake from coiling, which it must do in order to strike. Because of this the Indian declares that the eagle possesses the power to charm the snake by flying above it and gently caressing it with his wings.[59]

Father Dumarest describes the eagle trap used at Cochiti to catch the birds alive. The hunter is concealed in a deep and wide hole which has been covered with brush. A rabbit is placed over the opening for bait. In the bottom of the hole is a bowl filled with water in which the eagle

---

PLATE 11. *Half mask, made of a strip of leather with a beard of horsehair.*   ⟫→

Plate 11

is mirrored as it circles overhead. The hunter can thus watch its movements, and when the bird swoops down upon its prey he reaches through the brush and makes it captive.[60]

In the western pueblos young eagles are stolen from the nests. At Hopi there are even property rights[61] in eagles, and clan-owned nests are watched so that one small bird can be taken from the brood and the rest left unharmed. Live eagles, and macaws also, are kept in cages[62] on the housetops or in shelters at the side of the village. Even in Coronado's day "there were also tame eagles, which the chiefs esteemed to be something fine."[63]

Duck.—The feather of the wild duck is often spoken of as the "looking back" or "turn around" feather.[64] Its iridescence adds beauty to any ornament. Although the wild duck is not significant in myth or religion in all the villages, Hopi, Zuñi, Isleta, San Felipe, and Jemez appear to hold this bird sacred. At Zuñi it is said that the supernaturals assume the form of the duck in order to swim the river to the Sacred Lake, their home.[65]

Crow and owl.—The crow and the owl are two birds of adverse symbolism. Bad fortune accompanies the "kaa, kaa" of the crow. He is the persistent thief who follows the sower and then himself makes his thieving known. He is often associated with witchcraft,[66] and always with bad luck.* Certain Zuñi kachinas wear collars of crow or raven feathers (pl. 5). These frighten the children as well as drive away bad luck.[67] The owl is often symbolic of witches and witchcraft, probably because of its nocturnal habits.[68] We sometimes find bunches of owl feathers used as decoration on kachina masks.

The "summer birds."—All those which are brightly colored, as, for example, the jay, red hawk, road runner, bluebird, oriole, and humming-bird,[69] often have some special significance. The oriole, or chat, is the bird of the north since yellow is the north color, and the blue jay supplies the priest with feathers which he is entitled to wear in his hair on ceremonial occasions.[70] These small birds are caught in traps of horsehair

---

* At Laguna and Zuñi.

and sticks,[71] or on a plant called "crowfoot." They are kept in small cages on the housetops.

Many feathers are connected with special persons or incidents. The downy eagle feather dyed red (pl. 7) is a sign of the priesthood at Zuñi.[72] The sparrow hawk is associated with the Black Eye, a priest-clown group at Isleta, while the Koshare, another group, use the turkey.[73]

To an Indian the downy white feather is very close to life itself. "The feather is the pictorial representation of the breath," and "breath is the symbol of life."[74] There is hardly an act of ritual or drama without the use of feathers, and all feathers for ceremonial use must come from the living bird.[75]

Feathers on the prayer-plume offerings planted at almost all the villages were supposed to "provide clothing for the supernaturals."[76] Just as food, accompanied with a prayer, is sent to the other world when it is cast into the fire or into the river, so these feathers are sent to clothe the Great Ones.[77] At Jemez the erect turkey feathers bound at the back of the prayer stick represent the red-and-blue-bordered white Hopi blanket[78]— a recognition in form and pattern of an actual garment. More often the stipulated arrangement of feathers on the prayer stick is a matter of ritual form and the resulting kachina costumes do not bear a relationship to their supposed origin. At all events, it is true that the kachinas are conspicuous for their beautiful feather ornaments.

Each particular rite or entertainment has its specified method by which feather ornamentation is employed. Sometimes the feathers are painted, in a stylized manner, on the articles or emblems used in the rite; this obviously was taken over from its origin in basket and pottery decoration. We find them also on a tablita form over a mask, and on the cheek of an unmasked dancer.[79]

Aside from the robe so often indicated on the Shalako Kachina doll, feathers are used on ceremonial costumes purely as ornamentation. Single feathers are hung alone or in groups from belts and arm bands (pl. 35) by buckskin thongs or homespun cotton cord. They are often tied to the corners or centers of kilts and blankets (pl. 7). Headdress and mask ornaments are made of feathers fashioned together in various patterns. Accessories (pl. 30), either worn or carried, are peripherally trimmed with feathers or made of feathers entirely.

The methods of application vary. The quill may be tied on with buckskin, yucca, or cotton cord. Cornhusks may be folded and wrapped tightly around the quill end, making a holder. Buckskin may be used in the same manner. Holes may be bored in gourds, corncobs, or wood, and feathers stuck into them. Down is even applied to horsehair and wool with a syrup made by boiling the juice of the yucca fruit.

When colored feathers are not available, the white ones are stained the desired colors. Downy eagle feathers are dyed red to indicate membership in societies. Furthermore, since feathers naturally lend themselves to varied and graceful forms of ornamentation, it is only the rigid rules prescribed by ritual which prevent artist creators from making endless objects in this medium. As a consequence, new forms are created only when a new character is introduced, and ordinarily the same ornaments differ only as the ability of one craftsman exceeds that of another.

When not in use, sacred feathers are kept carefully packed in special boxes, made of cottonwood, which have ingenious sliding lids held in place by fitted pegs. At Jemez the sacred feathers are laid away wrapped simply in buckskin.[80] Each ornament and feather is renewed and redecorated for every dance series; for many days before a performance the priest works secretly with others within the kivas to get them ready. With this constant renewal of parts and the variability of human craftsmanship, it is small wonder that the forms change despite the fact that the artist has carefully followed a specified plan. In the work of renovation only hand-spun cotton cord can be used, as that has a sacred significance. Cornhusk is used as a firm base upon which feathers can be fastened, or it may be wrapped around the quill to hold the feathers in a rigid position.

There is an interesting headdress in the Buffalo Dance (fig. 25, p. 189). It consists of a white deerskin band about two and one-half inches wide, on the right side of which is fastened a black buffalo horn and on the left a fan of six eagle tail feathers firmly bound with cornhusk and tied in place with a buckskin thong at right angles to the quill ends.[81]

Feathers are used on other parts of costumes. Buckskin shields worn on the back may be edged with feathers or have some special feather treatment at top or bottom. Again, eagle feathers are sewn to deerskin or cornhusk bands which follow the arm contour from neck to wrist to provide the wings of the eagle dancers. Fan-shaped tail ornaments of eagle feathers are also made.

In the ceremonial dances, various articles carried by the dancers are distinguished by the feathers attached to them. The presiding priest carries a special feather wand to indicate his position and the particular office which he is performing.

NATURE FORMS

A great wealth of economic and aesthetic material is found by the Indian in the plants and trees that grow on every side. Roots, stems, leaves, and fruit give variously of food, medicines, and clothing. Certain of the initiated are believed to be blessed with the power to communicate with the plant world. Many plants are held sacred, "for some of them were dropped to the earth by the Star People; some were human beings before they became plants; others were the property of the gods and all, even those from the heavens, are the offspring of the Earth Mother, for it was she who gave the plants to the Star People before they left the world and became celestial beings."[82]

Fir, oak, cottonwood, corn, and squash supply names for clans and individuals. In the clanless villages where the two-moiety division is found, "Squash" is applied to the group of Summer people and "Turquoise"

PLATE 12. *Face mask. The nearest approach to realism.*   ⟫→

Plate 12

to the Winter people: the one suggesting summer sun and growth; the other, winter cold and storms from the sky.

In order to satisfy his aesthetic urge, man has always bedecked himself in season with blossom, fruit, or leaf as the form or color has pleased his eye or enhanced his beauty. No discussion of the costumes of the Pueblo Indian would be complete without reference to these nature forms, which, though as used may be in either the fresh or the cured state, have come originally from living plants and trees.

Evergreen.—The most conspicuous nature form, and that regarded with the greatest reverence, is the spruce tree and its branches. In special rain ceremonies the Rain priests and the dancers who personate the Rain Makers address the spruce trees, invoking them to extend their arms (referring to the branches) and water the earth. The breath from the gods of the undermost world is supposed to ascend through the trunks of these trees and form clouds behind which the Rain Makers work.[83] The Douglas spruce is the most desired[84] and great effort is often made to obtain it from the deep canyons of the mountainous country where it grows. Among the Tewa, officials go out the day before the ceremony to bring back its branches. In some of the performances small trees are set up in the plaza after midnight and the next day are worked into the dance pattern. At Hopi, spruce is more difficult to obtain. A runner is sent to bring it from the mountains, and this takes from early morning till late at night. At Hopi, also, the branches are planted and the children are amazed, when they awaken, to find "trees" growing in the plaza—a phenomenon explained as one which accompanies the supernaturals who are about to dance there.

Performers wear sprigs of spruce stuck in the belt, and in arm bands, and sprigs are carried in the hands. Small branches are tied together with yucca cord to form anklets (pl. 6) and great collars (pl. 4). Occasionally, spruce forms part of a headdress or fills in the back of a mask. Spruce branches are never thrown promiscuously about after ceremonial use;

they are dropped over the cliff or into the river, or are buried in the sands at the river's edge to be washed downstream with the next floodwater.

Used on the ceremonial costume in the summer dances, evergreen is the symbol of life. Green yarns embroidered on kilts and ceremonial blankets have the same connotation.

If spruce cannot be obtained, juniper may be substituted as an evergreen. Firebrands are made from juniper bark, since it burns very slowly and thus is a good means of transporting live coals. Torches of juniper are carried in night ceremonies. At Santa Clara and at Hopi a special Old Man is impersonated by the wearing of a juniper-bark cap or headdress.

Gourds.—The gourd was one of the aboriginal plants cultivated by the Pueblo Indian before the advent of the Spaniards. It has an important place in both their ceremonial and domestic lives. The gourd, in fact, is indispensable to the Pueblo Indian; it is a bucket, a dipper, or a bowl as the need arises. Several species were grown. Some were small, some were long-necked, and others grew flat or round. By running the vine on a pole so that the green fruit hung down it was possible to develop extremely long, thin gourds; and it was possible to flatten them out by placing a weight on one side. Under stimulating conditions very large gourds have been grown. There are two masks made of gourds in the Museum of the American Indian, Heye Foundation.[85] One of them is large enough for a man to wear. With the lower end cut off, it would go over his head and rest upon his shoulders. There were holes for eyes and mouth. A smaller gourd made the snout, and the features were painted on. The other mask could have been worn by a boy.

The shell of the gourd is scraped clean of seeds and pulp and then thoroughly dried. As the gourd is a material more easily worked than wood, and, for the Hopi and the Zuñi, much more easily available, it is made into snouts and beaks and ear bobs for masks. A large number of these are kept on hand at all times, to be available for any dance ceremonies. Rarely, two gourds will grow so much alike that the necks can be used as horns on an animal mask. When several are found of the same size and shape, they are carved into flowers to decorate a headdress or arm bands. The heads of the sacred Plumed Serpents are made of gourds.[86] The mouth is cut to show two rows of teeth, between which a red leather tongue is allowed to dangle. Gourds are made into rattles, round or flat, with the necks serving as handles (fig. 20, p. 146). Certain phallic devices are made of the long variety of gourds and these symbolize fructification.[87]

Yucca.—Yucca, or Spanish bayonet, is a low-growing desert shrub. Its sharp, pointed leaves branch out stiffly from a single stem. The blossoms are white and appear in a cluster on a shoot several feet above the leaves. This plant is called "soapweed," and because it produces an excellent lather it is indispensable to the desert Indian. The roots are crushed or pounded with a stone and put into cold water to steep. Within a few moments a thick lather can be produced by brisk stirring. The fibrous

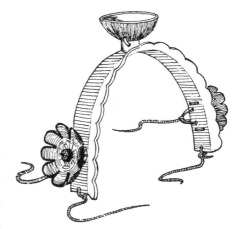

FIGURE 13. Headdress with flowers made of gourds.

parts are removed and the shampoo or laundry is ready. The glossy black hair which is a source of great pride to every Indian man, woman, and child is washed as often as once a week with this soap lather. No ceremony is complete without hair washing. Among the Hopi every infant when it is named, every girl on her marriage day, every boy upon initiation into a secret fraternity or a medicine society—all must have their hair washed. Before a public entertainment every dancer, and indeed every person in the village, is expected to wash his hair. At the conclusion of a ceremony every impersonator is discharmed—that is, the supernatural spirit which he has assumed is washed away in the shampoo and he becomes human once more. In all these ceremonies the yucca suds represent clouds. Ceremonial bowls full of suds are often found on the altars; they are imitation magic denoting that clouds are wanted to bring rain.

The long, flat leaves of the giant yucca are carried by warriors and whipping impersonators (pls. 5, 6, 35, 36).[88] Initiates are purified by whipping.[89]

The costumes of certain kachinas of the Hopi have skirts made of stiff yucca leaves.

Corn.—Everything connected with corn is sacred. For the Pueblo Indian, life itself depends upon the growth of corn. Since the beginning of time it has been his greatest source of food. Directly and indirectly his entire existence is related to the culture of corn. Land is owned by individual or tribal group, but wealth depends upon the production of corn. Soil and water are of prime importance because they make possible its growth. The Pueblo Indian believes that rain and snow are sent by the supernaturals and can be obtained only by prayer and ceremony, and thus have come into being the Weather Control groups which form the underlying structure of Pueblo life.

As the staple food, corn is eaten fresh or is dried and stored for the future. The need of safe storage space has had its influence upon the structure of house and village. As the basis of Pueblo life is corn, it is not surprising to find it a conspicuous feature of the ceremonial life. The perfect ear, with its special covering, is the life fetish of each individual, and is often placed upon the society altars or worn secreted in the belts of the dancers. Ears of appropriate colors are laid around the medicine bowl before the altar. The bowl represents the center and the corn the six cardinal directions.

White corn meal, finely ground, is the women's special offering, equivalent to the prayer plume of the men. However, both men and women sprinkle corn meal on the dancers. The priest sprinkles a 'road' into the dance plaza for the impersonators to follow, or with meal he designates

PLATE 13. *Helmet mask, Hopi Pawika. Occult symmetry achieved through fixing of ornaments.* ⟫→

Plate 13

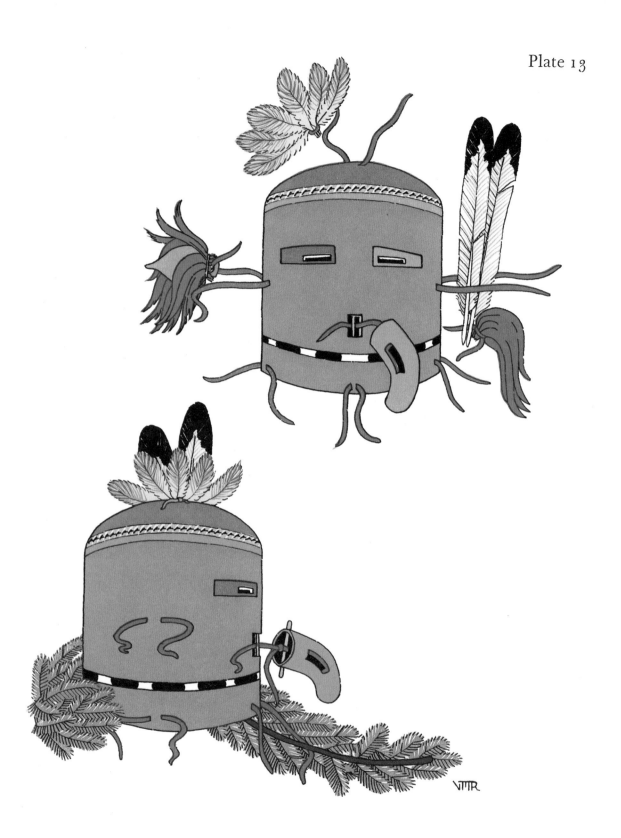

the 'way' to the edge of the village, where the populace go to offer prayers to the Sun. At the end of the Hopi Snake Dance the women describe a great circle with corn meal. The snakes used in the dance are heaped in the center of this circle; then, after another prayer and a sprinkling of meal, each member of the Snake Dance group grasps as many of the wriggling reptiles as he can and dashes away in one of the cardinal directions

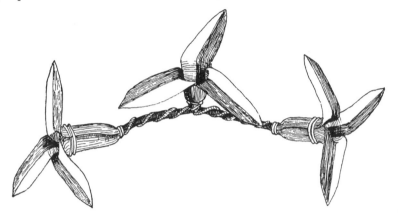

FIGURE 14. Cornhusk flowers worn by Powamu dancers, Hopi.

to deposit his burden far out on the desert, whence it is to return to the world below carrying to the gods the prayers for rain.

Corn in various forms is carried or worn by the dancers. Sometimes it is the actual ear, sometimes the symbolic representation of it—both three-dimensional and painted. Cornhusks are used, and even the cob. The whole grains are always carried somewhere on a dancer's person to symbolize prayers which accompany the dance. The knobs of the masks worn by the clown Mudheads have corn and other seeds tied in them.

Ears of corn are often carried by impersonators and women dancers as an accessory to their parts, or they are attached to the tablita worn by the maidens. The Sio Shalako mana, the Zuñi Shalako Maiden of Hopi, is shown with a stylized ear of corn on the forehead (pl. 18). Painted representations are found on masks, head boards, and tablets which are carried in each hand. The corncob is useful as a holder into which the feather quills are stuck, thus forming a feather bouquet. I have seen an example of a curved cob, stained from black at one end to red at the other, used as a beak on a mask.[90]

The dried husk is a useful part of the corn. It is slit into ribbons and used to decorate the hair (pl. 39) and caps of the clowns.[91] Balls of husk are covered with cotton cord at the head of the long fringe on the plaited ceremonial sash,[92] representing corn and rain and the desire for bountiful crops. Tightly twisted cornhusks form the framework and mounts for feathers in many ornaments. Cornhusks wound into a circlet may be worn on the head to support wooden symbols of lightning and clouds.[93] Skillful arrangements of cornhusks simulate teeth and mouths on masks. Cornhusks are rolled into cones and used as earbobs, or are fashioned into collars at the bottom of masks. Erna Fergusson colorfully describes the manufacture of gay cornhusk flowers: "They smoothed the pale gold husks on their knees, tore them into the right shape, and then, dipping twisted yucca fiber into shallow pottery bowls, they applied a light-red paint to one half of each leaf. The work was apparently negligently done, while conversation went on, but the results were beautiful. Soon four petals were ready, and then they were quickly twisted into the shape of a big open flower, like a squash blossom, tied, and laid aside. Without any apparent effort or hurry each man soon had beside him a pile of pale-gold and red blossoms."[94]

Cotton.—I have discussed the spinning and weaving of cotton into fabric, but with the Indian its ceremonial use does not stop there. It has a place in almost every ritual. The Zuñi name for unspun cotton is "down," and down, as I have said, is the sacred feather of life, the breath of the supernatural. It symbolizes clouds[95] and snow and is often stuck on the horsehair beards in place of eagle down. The tops of certain masks are covered with raw cotton to indicate that those gods are associated with rainmaking. Handmade cotton cord is always used in prayer plumes and for the purpose of fastening together feathers used for ornaments on the ceremonial costumes. It is placed across a road leading into the village to indicate that a ceremony is taking place. We often find the loosely twisted cord hanging from the crown of a wig in definite contrast to the black hair (pls. 3, 17).

Herbs and flowers.—The Pueblo plant forms are limited to those which will grow in a land of much sunshine and little rain. However, these are numerous. And since it was not always possible to travel great distances for herbs and leaves, the Indian was forced to employ that which was near at hand.

In wide desert spaces, colors and plant forms, flower and leaf, stand out in brighter shapes and make a more poignant appeal to the aesthetic sense. The sagebrush, the sunflower, are not homely, commonplace; they are vivid and beautiful. I remember the blanket-wrapped form of a young man who impulsively rushed out of the sacred dance room to pluck the sunflowers across the barbed wire fence and carried them back into the shadow of the dark kiva. When the dancers emerged a few minutes later to take their places in the dance pattern, each carried with the sprig of evergreen the nodding, golden heads of the sunflower. This was not a conventional part of the paraphernalia of the dance; it was evidence of that fundamental, primal thing which those who live close to nature so readily feel. The feathery pigweed may be carried and tossed to the spectators who line the edge of the plaza. Sagebrush adds a soft gray-green to the hand tablet of the Corn Maidens, and sand grass gives a brittle edge to tablita and wand. Mouse-leaf blossoms mixed with ocher earth will color bodies yellow, and crushed barberries give them a purple hue. To each dancer, after he has dressed, are given the powdered flowers of the wild buckwheat in order to assure him grace. White primrose blossoms are rubbed over the necks and arms of those who impersonate the Zuñi Corn Maidens, so that they may dance well and please the "white shell mother of the Sun Father" who will surely send rains to moisten the earth and make the corn grow.

DECORATION

When primitive man first sought to make himself attractive, he chose from his environment objects which were bright or colorful and wore them in his hair, strung them about his neck, looped them about his middle, or otherwise applied them to his person where application was possible. Garments evolved from this desire for ornamentation of the body and were used as protection from the elements or the immodest eyes of men. Hilaire Hiler points out that "ornament often exists without clothing, but clothing seldom, if ever, exists without ornament."[96]

Articles of clothing of the Pueblo Indian are the bases upon which the arts of the painter, the dyer, the embroiderer, and the weaver are practiced. Garment ornamentation is achieved through painting in pigment directly upon the surface of the fabric, the application of colored yarns or other materials by embroidery or appliqué, and the weaving of variously dyed yarns into a patterned fabric.

The effect of ornamentation varies with the method and the material used. Heavy embroidery raises the surface and stiffens the garment in the area in which it is applied, and painted designs may cause a cloth to hang rigid because of the adhesive matter used to make the pigment cling to the surface. On the other hand, a cloth made of dyed yarn may not vary at all from its uncolored prototype, since the pigment, though changing the color, does not affect the physical character of the cloth.

Color.—Since love of color is an inborn trait of the human race, it is not surprising to find the Pueblo Indian of the Southwest exercising it, albeit unconsciously. Colors abound in his kingdom of sandy space and limitless sky. The earth shows a myriad hues, played upon incessantly and with endless change by the brilliant sunlight or the passing clouds. The sky exhibits the pageantry of all those shifting forms of day and night, summer and winter, fair weather and foul, which are called the elements.

PLATE 14. *Basketry mask. Feathers are held in place by a braid of cornhusk.*   ⟫→

Plate 14

The parade of color passes from the pale iridescence of dawn through the white noon to the golden flamboyance of sunset, and on into the crisp blue-black of the star-pierced night. It is seen in the red and purple where the watercourse has gashed the mesa side; in the brittle-edged clumps of dark green piñon against a golden monotone of rolling sand; in the soft gradations of green and silver sagebrush and cactus-strewn flats; and on the great rolling mesa tops where blankets of purple lupin and yellow sulphur flowers have been carelessly flung across the sweep of space. The Indian had but to step to his housetop to see around and above him all these wonders of nature. He began very early to relate them to certain phases of his life.

Out of these associations grew a kind of symbolism in which color represented ideas and objects, mythical and real alike. Colors were related to the six directions: yellow to the north, blue to the west, red to the south, white to the east, many colors to the zenith, and black to the nadir. The origin of these associations is clothed in mystery.* It is obvious that yellow colors the sky to the north before the angry winter storms sweep down from the mountains, and it has been suggested that the Pacific Ocean to the west accounts for the blue.[97] Red is applied to the south because of the ruddy warmth of summer, and white to the east because it suggests early morn and the rising sun.[98] The many colors of the zenith reflect the sky from which all colors come, and the nadir is black because of the dark inner worlds from which in myth the Pueblo peoples emerged.

Paralleling these directional hues are the colored ears of corn used on the altars and incorporated into the legendary background of the social and religious life. Certain of the supernaturals are characterized in sets which correspond to the cardinal directions and colors. During ceremonies these supernaturals appear in the masks and body paint of their world quarters. The Zuñi Salimapiya[99] are an interesting example of one of these

---

* Some of the pueblos either lack this association altogether or have a variant. "Taos appears to have no directional association with color" (Parsons, 1936a, p. 105). In Isleta only five directions are recognized and there the colors are: east, white; north, black; west, yellow; south, blue (Parsons, 1932, p. 284).

series (pls. 5, 6). There are twelve of them, two for each direction. They appear together only once every four years; at other times two of them, each of a different color, may be seen simultaneously. The black may appear with the many-colored, representing respectively the nadir and the zenith; again, the yellow may appear with the blue, representing the north and the west. In 1879 Matilda Stevenson saw two of these directional supernaturals at Zuñi, which she describes as follows:

"They represented the Zenith and Nadir, the one for Zenith having the upper portion of the body blocked in the six colors, each block outlined with black. The knees and the lower arms to the elbow have the same decoration; the right upper arm is yellow, the left blue; the right leg is yellow, the left blue. Wreaths of spruce are worn around the ankles and wrists. The war pouch and many strings of grain of black and white Indian corn hung over the shoulder, crossing the body. The upper half of the Salimapiya of the Nadir is yellow and lower half black; the lower arms and legs and feet are yellow, the upper arms and legs black. He wears anklets and wristlets of spruce, a war pouch, and strings of black and white corn."[100]

Ruth Bunzel, writing in 1932, says the Blue Salimapiya "has his mask painted with blue gum paint, his body with the juice of black cornstalks . . . thighs white . . . he wears a special kilt called the Salimapiya kilt. It is embroidered like the ceremonial blanket with butterflies and flowers."[101] He also wears a blue leather belt and spruce anklets, and his feet are bare.

The impression of the general public, when viewing Indian motifs in costumes and decoration, is that they are composed of purely symbolic patterns. This is rarely true. Many designs are used only for decoration, and if by chance they symbolize an object, quality, or idea, it is merely by association. The emotional response to color association differs with the group, and what becomes a symbol to one group remains only a decoration with another.

Green suggests grass, and it may mean life and fecundity. Blue-green is reverently used, as it is always associated with the sky. It is a 'valuable' color and of great religious import. The blue prayer stick is male and connotes the sun; the yellow represents the female and the moon. The turquoise stone is regarded with great reverence and the wealth of a man is displayed by the quantity of turquoise he wears about his neck. "Yellow on the face represents corn pollen, and brings rain,"[102] and yellow body paint is used by the Squash groups or Summer people. On the other hand, "red paint on the body is for the red-breasted birds, and the yellow paint for the yellow-breasted birds, and for the flowers and butterflies and all the beautiful things in the world," and again, "the spots of paint of different colors . . . are the raindrops falling down from the sky,"[103] or those same spots may represent the drops of blood of a little boy who, in a myth, was killed by the supernaturals. They ever afterward wore the spots on their masks.[104]

From the frequency with which designs are repeated on like objects, and the same colors used, one can be certain that there is a definite symbolic pattern for the ceremonial use of color. We do not know whether the source of this symbolism is known to others besides the priests who prescribe it and who have acquired their knowledge from priests of the preceding generation.

The association of color is one thing, the application another. The range of hues used by the Pueblo Indian was limited to the colors that were available and to the manners in which they could be used. Materials were colored by three methods: dyeing, a process by which a permanent union is brought about between the material to be dyed and the coloring matter applied to it; staining, a method by which colored particles become entangled in the surface of the fiber but can be removed by washing or rubbing; and painting, by which a pigment is applied to the surface. McGregor says:

"Dyes or pigments used in coloring yarns or fabrics may be divided into two general classes: organic and inorganic. In prehistoric cotton fabrics the inorganic dyes are by far the most common, and consist largely of three colors: red, produced from hematite or some other iron oxide; yellow, from a yellow ochre; and blue or green, produced from copper sulphate. These inorganic dyes may be readily determined by a superficial examination with a medium-powered microscope, for the dye material does not penetrate the fiber but clings to it in the form of grains. Organic dyes seem to consist of only black, dark brown, and a light blue. These dyes are relatively permanent and cannot be washed out, as can the inorganic types."[105]

Paints and stains.—The processes of painting and staining which employ inorganic pigments are used to color the face and body, articles made of skin, wood, and nature forms, and certain fabrics for which the required colors cannot be obtained in permanent dyes.

These earth colors are found in the mountains and valleys surrounding each pueblo. Most of the villages are thus able to obtain their own supplies, but often color in the form of cakes or powder is obtained by trade with other Indians. The Zuñi procure their turquoise blue mask paint, ready for use, from the Santo Domingo because they believe the color is better.[106] Mrs. Parsons relates that a Jemez Indian once asked her to get some red face paint from the Hopi for him. "He said they had the best."[107] The hue of these pigments varies greatly with the locality in which they are found and the purity with which they can be obtained. A report on Acoma suggests that the original earth color is none too pure, but by separating the ground particles a fairly clear color is obtained. "A yellowish rock is ground fine and the dust mixed with water. The sediment is thrown away after being allowed to settle twice. The third accumulation of sediment is kept."[108]

Some colors come in rock form; others are a clay. "Iron tinged the earth red, brown, yellow, orange and intermediate shades. Copper produced

PLATE 15. *Mountain sheep mask, Hopi. Molded horns of deerskin carry symbols of clouds, rain, and lightning. The vizor is of basketry.* ⟫→

Plate 15

the blues and greens. Black came from iron and magnesium."[109] The pigment, from whatever source, is ground in a stone mortar or on a metate
with a mano. The process of grinding is often a special ceremony at
which the young girls are invited to do the grinding while the men sing
to them.[110] At other times the grinding is a secret rite and is done in the
kiva by the society head and his helpers.[111] The ground powder is mixed
with water and used directly, or it may be combined with an adhesive
substance, such as piñon gum or
the juice of yucca fruit,[112] to make
it more permanent. Another
method of fixing a permanent
color is to squirt over it a water
in which ground-up pumpkin
seeds have been steeped for a

FIGURE 15. Containers for pigments used in
painting ceremonial objects.

long time.[113] A shiny surface is made possible by mixing the paint with
yucca juice or the yolk or white of eggs.[114] A glaze of albumen from the
egg white may be applied over the paint,[115] or a spray of cow's milk blown
from the mouth makes the object bright and shiny.[116] Grease is mixed
with body paint to make it adhere and also to impart a sheen.[117]

Paints are applied with the fingers, a stick, or brushes of yucca fiber.
A piece of yucca leaf is selected and chewed to separate the fibers and
cleanse them. This makes a very good brush. A different brush is used
for each color. The pigments are mixed in small pottery cups made
specially in groups for that purpose and decorated with designs relating
to water and rain. Sometimes flower petals and shells are ground and
mixed with the powder to give it more 'power' or to make it more sacred.

Even today the paints for ceremonial purposes are of native make. It is
a rare and decadent society which permits the use of any commercial
paint on the masks, body, or dress of a dancer.

White is obtained from a white clay (kaolin) which is soaked in water
or ground and used as a powder—the counterpart of the fuller's earth, or

white clay paste, used by Greek and Roman artisans to cleanse and whiten their cloth. All white garments are treated with it before they are worn. This clay is found up and down the Rio Grande and is traded to the Zuñi by the Acoma.[118] Masks are always painted white before any other color is applied. This forms a ground coat to fill up pores and give a smooth surface. White is often used as a body paint or powder.[119]

Black may be obtained from various sources. A pigment in common use comes from an ore (pyrolurite, a hydrated oxide of manganese)[120] which is mined.[121] This is used on prayer sticks and masks. Chimney soot is also used, especially for the eyes of a mask—being, for that purpose, mixed with the yolk of an egg to produce a gloss.[122] Corncobs, carbonized and ground, make a highly valued paint for masks. At Zuñi, they are found in the ancient ruins and carefully preserved for this purpose. Similar to this is the charcoal of willow which, when ground, is mixed with water for a body paint.[123] Corn rust or fungus mixed with water is used especially for a body paint; mixed with yucca syrup, it makes a shiny black paint which is used for masks.[124] An iridescent blackish substance ("black shiny dirt") is found in the water washes after a rain. It is probably the fine grains of quartz, sphalerite, and galena, the last-named being a ground concentrate of zinc ore.[125] This is mixed with grease and applied to the body, or it is mixed with yucca juice or piñon gum and applied to masks. Masks are also made to shine by the use of mica (micacious hematite), which is applied over black with some form of adhesive.[126]

Pink is a body paint used especially by the sacred clowns, the Mud-heads (pl. 40), and by the Kokochi and other masked gods.[127] It is a clay* obtained by the Zuñi from the shores of the Sacred Lake where the kachinas live. Every four years a pilgrimage is made there to secure it. It is kept in chunks until wanted, and then is wet with the tongue and rubbed on the body or mask.

The reds and yellows are ochers or oxides of iron. These rock forma-

---

* Kaolinite or a similar hydrated silicate of alumina.

tions, hematite and limonite, constitute the rugged edges of the mesa and the weird towering shapes that stand, massive and solitary, on the desert throughout all the great distance from the Grand Canyon to the Rio Grande.[128] Certain cliffs or mounds produce colors of greater purity than others do, and these the Indians have mined for centuries. One cave on the north side of the Grand Canyon produces a fine red ocher which is traded to the Hopi by the Shivwits, a tribe of Indians who dwell to the north.[129] Other mines are within easy reach of all the pueblos. The red is generally ground on a stone with water until the water becomes red. It can be used directly on the masks or the body. If light red is desired, the red water is mixed with pink or white clay. At Zuñi the yellow ocher is ground with the petals of yellow summer flowers (the buttercup) and abalone shells. This makes a very potent 'medicine.' When mixed with water, it becomes a sacred paint.[130] Another yellow is made of corn pollen. When mixed with the boiled yucca juice, it produces a glossy paint. It is thought to be flesh color.[131] At Laguna the faces of the dead are painted with corn pollen.

The most important color is turquoise. This blue-green paint is an oxidized copper ore (azurite and malachite in a calcite matrix).[132] It is found in the mountains to the east of the Rio Grande and is traded by the pueblos of those regions to the Hopi and Zuñi. Cakes or balls of this color are made by grinding the ore to a fine powder, mixing it with water, and boiling with piñon gum. The cakes can then be put away and kept indefinitely. A method of painting masks at Acoma with this pigment is described as follows: "One puts some of this substance into his mouth with eagle feathers, chews it for some time, then blows it onto the mask. The breath is expelled with it, giving the effect of a spray."[133]

There are also stains from plants which are used to color the body. Pink is produced by boiling wheat with a small sunflower,[134] and purple can be obtained from the chewed stalks and husks of black corn. An example is seen on the body of the blue-masked Salimapiya (pl. 6). The purple obtained from crushing the berries of barberry is used on the body and for painting ceremonial objects.[135]

Dyes.—The organic colors or dyes of the Pueblo were very limited. Certain trees and bushes yielded colors that were used to dye the yucca fibers, but with the advent of cotton the process became difficult. It is a well-known fact that cotton is the hardest of all fibers to dye. Specimens of native dyed cotton are rare and the colors are always drab and faded. It appears, then, that the prehistoric Pueblo people had no cotton garments of strong colors, and this made the need of brilliant ornamentation imperative.

Brown dye could be obtained from alder bark, dried and finely ground. It was boiled until it became red, and then was cooled. Deerskin soaked overnight in this liquid turned a brilliant red-brown. This was the favorite color for moccasins (pl. 33), Hopi fringed leather kilts, arm bands, bandoleers, and anything fashioned of deerskin. Sometimes the alder bark was chewed, and the juice ejected upon the deerskin, which was then rubbed between the hands.[136] Cotton cloth took only a small quantity of this dye and turned reddish tan.

A blue dye was made from the seeds of sunflowers.[137]

New colors came with the introduction and use of wool. Woolen fibers take dye much more readily than cotton. By this time the Navaho had learned the art of weaving from the Pueblo Indian. Alongside this knowledge of weaving there developed a new method of dyeing, as is evidenced by the well-known Navaho blankets. Unquestionably there was borrowing back and forth between the two groups. It is possible to say, then, that the Pueblo native dyes were similar to those of the Navaho.[138] These dyes were made from the leaves, stems, and roots of plants and shrubs and certain earth fillers, with use of piñon gum and a mordant of juniper ashes to make the color lasting. There were black, dark red, green, and

PLATE 16. *Humis mask, Hopi. The terraced tablet over the helmet is decorated with symbols of the rainbow and germinated seed.*   ⟫⟫→

Plate 16

the various yellows. From time to time indigo was imported from Mexico, along with other dyestuffs.

Since 1880, good commercial aniline dyes have largely taken the place of the native colorings. It is now rare to find a woolen blanket colored with native dyes, and even rarer to find, on cotton cloths, woolen embroidery which is native dyed. I have seen a few specimens in museums and private collections. The native dyes are soft and exquisite in their beauty. Once these are seen, the modern greens and reds appear harsh and overbrilliant.

Embroidery.—Pueblo Indian embroidery is a pure form of ceremonial decoration. It is found on dance kilts, ceremonial mantles (pls. 7, 22), and the dresses made of hand-woven strips of cotton cloth (pl. 1). Occasionally the ordinary blue woolen dresses are embroidered with simple borders. The designs are highly conventionalized and dynamically abstract, with bold forms and geometric patterns.

"The art of embroidery as now practiced is a fairly recent one and is probably an outgrowth of the painting on kilts mentioned by Espejo or of the raised patterns found in weaving."[139] It is probable that no needlework decoration was done by the Pueblo Indians before the coming of the white man, since no examples are extant which do not utilize woolen yarn. It was the white man who brought the sheep. The yarns employed today are almost always commercial yarns or aniline-dyed hand-spun wool.

Rectangles of white cotton cloth, equal in size, are made into ceremonial mantles and dresses; one is worn hanging from the shoulders, the other is fastened around the body and held with a belt. They are similar to the wedding robe of the Hopi bride, which is completely white. It is later embroidered by her husband or a male relative for her use in ceremonies.[140] The same style of robe is made for god impersonators and priests. The decoration motif at the bottom "takes the form of a broad band of black wool with two vertical stripes of green appearing at intervals. On these broad borders the only space not completely covered is

a thin meandering line of the white cotton base which appears diagonally crossing the black and green. This white design-line creates a strong
off-balance movement to the general vertical embroidery, seeming to
exaggerate the movement of the dance in which it is used."[141] The upper
edge of this band is terraced, and frequently through its center may be
seen diamond-shaped medallions with designs of clouds, rain, squash
flower, and butterfly symbols[142]—brilliant jewels of color. The design motif may differ among the pueblos, but the effect is always the same. The
upper border is narrower and has only the green stripes and white meandering lines to break its solidity.

The rectangular dance kilts are also made of white cotton cloth and
embroidered with various patterns. The Hopi type has a vertical band
in black, red, and green up and down the two short sides. A special Zuñi
type has a wide border similar to the mantle, with terraced top and colored medallions. It is worn by the Salimapiya. Other kilts have designs
and borders which vary according to pueblo and impersonation.

In the earlier days a few of the women's woolen dresses were embroidered. The Zuñi used a deep blue woolen yarn in identical designs on
the upper and lower borders,[143] and at Acoma they embroidered similar
borders in color.[144]

Most of the embroidery for the Pueblos is done by the Hopi men, who
are also the weavers. Special orders are filled for the priests of other
pueblos who want mantles or kilts for their ceremonies. "Hopi embroidery—an art practiced only by men—is governed by very rigid rules."[145]
The patterns are traditional and can be easily recognized on any dancer.

During the process of embroidery the cloth is stretched on a frame
made of sticks with pointed ends.[146] The pattern is never indicated on
the cloth, but is built up by counting threads. The material is folded
for a center line and the border is worked in each direction so that it
will come out even.

In early days, bone awls were used to poke the yarn through the cloth;

now, steel darning needles have taken their place. A simple back stitch is used, leaving much thread on the right side and picking up only a few threads on the under side. The white meander lines are made by carrying the yarn under certain threads, leaving their natural white exposed.

Colored designs are incorporated in sash ends through the brocade weave (pl. 31). (This process was described in the section on weaving.) Limited by the warp and weft of the loom, these designs are geometric. Colors are worked into separate patterns. A characteristic diamond shape in the center of the panel is made up of a border and triangular sections. Above and below run bands of black, green, and blue, with white figures picked out in the basic weave.

In the anklet another decorative effect is achieved. An oblong piece of deerskin or leather is slit internally in narrow lengthwise strips, leaving the ends uncut. These strips are wound with colored wools in geometric patterns (pl. 24). Porcupine quills and horsehair create a similar pattern. The quills, with points cut off, are moistened to make them pliable. Slit or flattened by drawing between the teeth or over the thumbnail, they are folded around the leather strip and caught by a series of half hitches in the horsehair (pl. 8).[147] Today they are sewn in place by stitches through the center of the strip. When stained with soft bright colors from berries, roots, and flowers,[148] porcupine quills make exquisite designs with a mosaiclike quality. This is a method of decoration employed by the Plains Indians. It is probable that the Pueblos acquired the technique from them.

PART THREE

Detailed Analyses of Parts of Costumes

IN DECORATING the human body two methods are generally employed: painting the body in one or more colors, and hanging divers objects upon it. Body paint is the simplest—and it may have been the first—form of covering employed.[1] The origin of the idea of covering the body has been attributed variously to consciousness of sex, the ego, the aesthetic urge, and the desire for protection from the elements and from the evil spirits.[2] Today, the Pueblo Indian colors his body in patterns which he believes were dictated by his supernaturals. These pigments are supposed to set him apart from his ordinary, human self and to give him the immortality of the gods as long as he wears them in ceremony. He associates the colors with good and evil spirits, and he attributes special power to certain hues and pigments, not only because they are hard to obtain in his limited world of natural resources, but also because he believes that they act favorably upon the supernaturals when they are employed in the proper patterns, which are rigidly prescribed. Body coverings play an important role in all ceremonials, and certain body paints are associated with particular types of impersonations.

BODY PAINT

The colored pigments are considered the "most sacred part of a dancer's regalia,"[3] and their power is superseded only by the masks of the god impersonators. When these masks are omitted, the body paint is imbued

[109]

with their magical power. With the colored pigments on his body, the man is charmed as he goes through the ritual, and no one should touch him, for he is not of this world. At the end of the performance he must be discharmed and his human self returned to him by the ceremonial washing of his hair and body. Until this is accomplished he is not permitted to go to his home. At Zuñi this discharming rite is performed, for a kachina impersonator, by his mother or some female relative.[4]

Women performers and the male impersonators of the female deities are rarely colored except for their hands and feet. Generally, the upper torso and the arms and legs of the men are nude and thus provide space and form for a variety of designs and hues. The most frequently used colors are pink, red, and black; white, blue, purple, and yellow are seen occasionally. Colors are combined in patterns which are significant for a particular impersonation or ritual, or which constitute a conventional body design for a group or a pueblo. In the Corn Dance at Jemez the bodies of the men dancers were colored according to the moiety to which they belonged: orange for the Squash or Summer people, and blue for the Turquoise or Winter people.[5] One of the conventional patterns at Hopi for the body paint of the god impersonator is red on the torso and upper legs, with blue on the right shoulder and breast, the left lower arm, and the right lower leg. Yellow is on the left shoulder, the right lower arm, and the left lower leg, and two vertical lines of alternate blue and yellow run from breast to waist and from shoulder to elbow as well as around each knee (pl. 24). This may possibly bear some relation to the Indian conception of the duality of life, in which blue signifies female and yellow male. A similar pattern is found in which the whole body is black or red, with the shoulder, arm, and leg design in yellow (pl. 35).

At Zuñi a double row of dots from waist to shoulder and down the arm, front and back, represents drops of rain and at the same time tends

PLATE 17. *Upoyona mask, Zuñi. Three strands of cotton cord hang from a topknot of parrot and downy eagle feathers. The domino eye design is painted on.* ⟫→

Plate 17

to slenderize the figure.[6] "The loins are always painted white, regardless of whether kilt or breechcloth is worn. This is 'for the sun.' One inform-ant offered the explanation that the white paint was used to protect the light-colored clothing. When full costume is worn the whole body is said to be painted white."[7]

Sometimes the body is painted in halves,[8] divided medially with the right side, arm, and leg black, and the left white.[9] Marsden Hartley saw, in what he calls a "Mercy Dance," a "warm tawny reddish earth tone with black stripes painted tiger-like at intervals down the entire right half and the other half a light greenish hue."[10] Knees are painted red to suggest speed; runners in ceremonial races always have red-painted knees.[11]

The bodies of the Buffalo impersonators are painted black broken by white crosses (pl. 21), "the sign of the bow."[12] This same design is used to signify the track of the road runner, a bird which leaves a footprint so perplexing that it is not possible to determine in which direction it was traveling.[13]

All these body paints are made up of earth pigments and plant stains which do not require the use of a glue to make them adhere. Thus the mixture is not injurious to the body, as there is no foreign matter to clog the pores and prevent the natural breathing of the skin. The pigments are mixed with water and applied in the liquid state, so that there is no caking of the colored powders upon the skin. Corn smut is used for black, ochers for yellow and reds, clays for white and pinks, and oxide of copper ore for the turquoise color. Stains are applied by rubbing a fruit, like barberry, over the body, or by chewing the stalk or leaves of other plants and applying the fluid thus obtained.

MANTLES

The use of mantles over the shoulders, for the purpose of concealing and protecting the upper part of the body, is not common among male Pueblo actors. Whenever used, they signify a special character or a person of eminence. On the other hand, impersonators of female characters always wear some kind of blanket or shawl. The most prized is the embroidered white blanket (pl. 34), hand-woven from native cotton by the Hopi in a plain basket weave. This, minus the embroidery, is the specification for the large white robe of the Hopi bride. It is decorated in woolen yarns of black and green, with touches of red and yellow in the wide borders at the top and bottom, and the corners are finished with tassels of black yarn. It is whitened with a paste made of finely powdered white clay (kaolin) to keep it clean.[14] This blanket is a rectangle about four feet by five and one-half feet[15] and when used as a mantle is always worn over both shoulders.[16] This form of blanket is probably not prehistoric, since "no embroidered wedding blankets antedate the period when dyed yarns could be procured from the trader and all known specimens are worked with worsteds, but many were collected before aniline colors came into use. Of the character of the wedding blanket before wool was introduced there is no information, though following the method employed in the kilts of the snake society the garments may have been ornamented with painted designs."[17]

The Maiden's shoulder blanket is of white cotton with wide, dark blue, or dark blue and red, woolen borders woven on two ends (pl. 38). The weave is a diagonal twill, and the shawl measures thirty-six by forty-eight inches. It is worn either over both shoulders or over the left shoulder and under the right arm, and it is knotted in front. The over the left shoulder and under the right arm manner of wearing the shawl is the most common, as this leaves the right arm free from restriction. Formerly, most Pueblo girls wore this dress-up garment on festival days. Today it has been replaced by gaudy, printed Mexican squares or overbrilliant plaids of machine manufacture.

In dress for ceremonial occasions the Maiden's blanket is worn by impersonators[18] and by participants in the Women's Society rites and dances.

Formerly, an all black or dark blue woolen shoulder blanket served the women as an everyday dress. It was worn in the same manner as the Maiden's blanket, or over the head with the ends hanging in front or thrust behind the shoulders. Mrs. Stevenson says that even in 1879, when she made her first visit to the Southwest, "a Pueblo woman or child would no sooner appear without this special piece except in certain ceremonials than a civilized woman would leave off her dress."[19] Even today, women and girls wear some kind of shawl or scarf over their heads or around their shoulders, regardless of its incongruity with their American store clothes.[20] Some female impersonators wear these dark shawls in place of the Maiden's blanket. It is also not unusual to see them side by side in a long line of dancers. The shawl is of the same size and weave of material as that worn as a woman's dress.

Occasionally there are special mantles, such as the ancient, painted cotton cloth seen on the Aholi (pl. 30), or the Pueblo and Navaho woolen blankets worn by the leaders or chiefs. Certain personages may also wear, on occasion, one of the rare rabbitskin robes which are still in existence.

Deerskin and other dressed hides are variously worn, either over both shoulders or over the right shoulder and under the left arm. They are often untrimmed, with the leg pieces hanging but knotted so that they will not drag (pl. 33), or they may be shaped to make a rectangular or square garment. The pelt of a deer, mountain lion, goat, or sheep sometimes makes a shoulder cape[21] or small mantle to distinguish a character.

BODY GARMENTS

Breechclout.—The breechclout is the only undergarment worn by the men, both in everyday life and in ceremonies. It is used to protect the person even when trousers are worn. It is always worn under the dance kilt except by the Mudheads, the Zuñi clowns, who are "just like children"[22] and are symbolized in myth as supernaturals "in semblance of males, yet like boys, the fruit of sex . . . not in them."[23]

The size of the breechclout varies. In Taos it is broad and long, hanging nearly to the ground,[24] while in the west it is short and narrow, the ends merely folding over the belt, front and back. The most desired material for this garment is hand-woven cotton cloth, but dark blue native cloth is often used, and sometimes even the woven ceremonial sash itself is used, its gay-hued ends contributing greatly to the color of figure and dance.[25]

The ordinary breechclout often has fringed ends or ends finished with embroidery or bright cording in geometric patterns. Decorated ends form a design element in the costume when drawn out over the belt and allowed to hang free (pl. 35).

Kilt.—The most characteristic ceremonial garment is the kilt. The forms and materials for this garment are numerous, but most frequently the kilt is of white homespun cotton cloth in a plain basket weave. It is about fifty inches long and twenty inches wide; it is wrapped around the loins and held in place at the waist by a belt. Generally made by the Hopi, the kilt is decorated by them with two embroidered panels symbolizing rain, clouds, and life—a characteristic design which always follows the same pattern, in black, green, and red.[26] Other pueblos often purchase from them kilt lengths of the white cloth and embroider or paint them in their own designs.

A band of black about an inch wide is often embroidered or crocheted around the bottom of the kilt, with small black squares or terraced shapes breaking into the white body at intervals above this lower border. The entire kilt is sometimes outlined with a thread of black, thus giving the garment definite limitations and forming a thin line of accent.

Special kilts of white cotton are painted or stained in the desired colors and designs. It has been suggested that this is the original method of decorating all white cotton garments.[27] The Hopi Snake Dance kilt is the most noticeable example today. On a background of tawny red a black band

PLATE 18. *Sio Shalako Maiden, Hopi. Mask of one of the giant goddesses. The elaborate headdress of symbolic shapes is held together by pegs and thongs. (Reconstructed from an antique mask at the Laboratory of Anthropology, Santa Fe.)* ⟫→

Plate 18

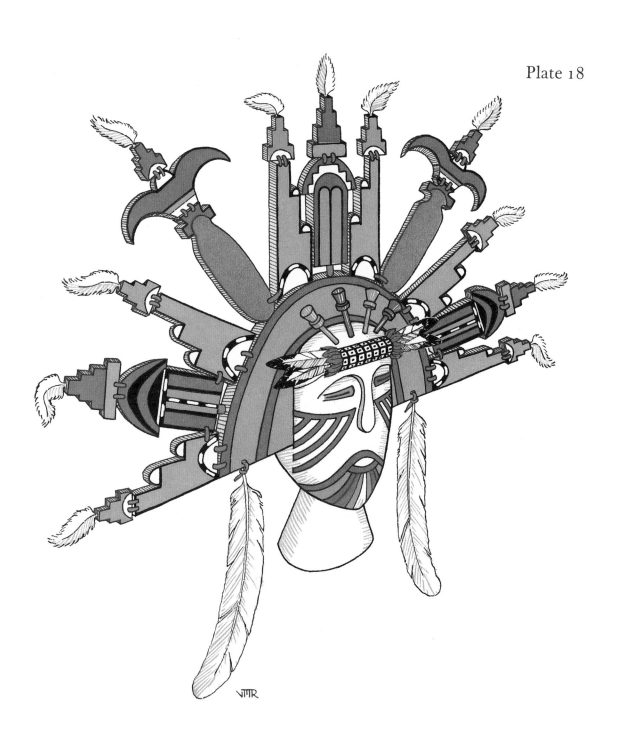

with white borders zigzags through the center, "representing the plumed snake, the arrow-shaped marks representing the footprints of ducks and short parallel marks representing the footprints of the frog, both water animals."[28] This serpent band is continuous, with neither head nor tail. At the bottom of the kilt are two lines of color, yellow and blue, bordered by black and white interrupted lines. A fringe of metal cones, useful as noisemakers, finishes the lower edge.[29] Painted cotton kilts are used by the Rio Grande Pueblos for their Buffalo Dances. These were probably preceded by kilts of deerskin bearing a similar design. Native cloth kilts, dark blue or black, are often seen. They have a straight band of red and green through the center and are characteristic of the impersonators of the Mountain Sheep and other Rio Grande personifications (pl. 26).

Occasionally the Maiden's shoulder blanket is folded in the center and worn as a kilt, with the dark border at the lower edge.[30] These kilts are most frequently worn with the opening on the right side; occasionally the embroidered ones are adjusted so that the panel comes to the back to be covered by the fringe of the plaited sash. There is possibly a symbolic relationship between this fringe and panel.

One other cloth garment of this type should command attention. It is called the Salimapiya kilt because it is worn especially by impersonators of those gods.[31] As there are openings up each side, this kilt is apparently made of two pieces, a front and a back. The bottom has a wide, embroidered border similar to that of the great mantle but with characteristic medallions of colored butterflies and flowers (pls. 5, 6).[32]

The deerskin kilt, similar to the white cotton garment, is worn by dancers associated with the hunt or with war. The most primitive form is a simple, untrimmed skin, with trailing legs knotted up around the bottom. It appears to have been but half a hide cut longitudinally. The peg holes made when the hide was cured can be seen along the irregular edges.[33] The trimmed deerskin kilt, either white or stained with earth colors, is a garment of great luxury today because of the scarcity of wild animals. A particular painted pattern found among the eastern pueblos has through the center a writing black serpent (pl. 21) with a plumed head and a tapering tail.[34] This is the symbol for the mystical being who lives in the earth, for "who can know her secrets so intimately as a serpent who penetrates her bosom?"[35] The pictured reptile may be surrounded by various symbols: the cross of the road runner, or signs representing the sun, moon,

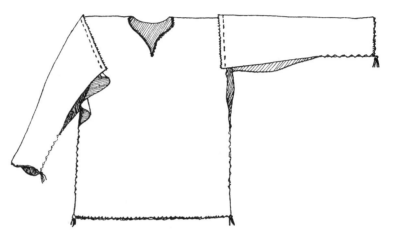

FIGURE 16. Pattern of shirt made of dark hand-woven wool. The sleeves are separate and sewed on the outside.

and stars. The lower edge is bordered in black and colored bands and around the ends of deerskin strips created by fringing the bottom are triangular tin pieces bent into cones. These replace the earlier animal-hoof and shell rattles with which these garments were formerly trimmed.

Special kilts are worn by certain dancers. One is fashioned of long horsehair stained red (pl. 35) and knotted on a cotton cord about the waist. It is held in place by a belt and hangs almost to the knee.[36] Another is made of long yucca leaves bound together on a single band, hanging straight and stiff in repose, but breaking and parting when the dancer is in motion.

Different materials or ornaments have been worn as overkilts. Narrow strips of cloth of a contrasting color, a fringe of leather, and a series of eagle feathers hung on deerskin thongs serve as examples.[37]

Shirt.—"The typical body garment of the Hopi man in historic times was a length of dark blue or black woolen cloth with an opening made in the middle for drawing over the head, equal lengths of the garment hanging over the back and front like the Mexican poncho."[38] With the addition of sleeves, this garment makes a distinguishing feature of a costume, being worn on the outside either with or without a belt. It was made of three pieces of flat cloth, the two sleeves sewn to the poncholike piece at each side midway down the length. Each side and the lower sleeves from wrist to elbow were sewn together with a simple running stitch. This left an opening under each arm minus a gusset—a pattern never fully understood by the Pueblos. They never mastered the art of cutting and fitting, but depended upon cloth in the piece, either rectangular or square. They created all their garments on geometrical lines, in contrast to the tailored garments of the skin-clothed Plains Indian. This cloth shirt was probably the successor to the deerskin shirt of the Plains; the deerskin shirt is believed to have been universally worn by the Pueblos when animals were more plentiful.

Two special shirts were introduced by the Spaniards and can be seen today among the eastern pueblos. At Isleta a garment of fine stuff, fulled to a yoke and with gathered sleeves, has a small flat collar and tight cuff of white embroidered material edged with a thin strip of red. From San Juan have come a few examples of crocheted garments of white cotton string with fringes down the underarm and sides, copying in modern materials the age-old leather garment of the Plains warrior.

Women's dress.—The ordinary dress of the Pueblo women is fashioned from a blanket of hand-woven woolen stuff which is dark brown, black, or blue. The brown and black are natural colors from the great number of brown and black sheep in the Indian flocks;[39] the blue was first obtained by dyeing the wool with indigo and later with aniline dyes.

This blanket is about four feet long and about three and one-half feet wide, a width sufficient to reach from the shoulder to the middle of the lower leg. The weave is a twill in which use is made of the diagonal pattern for the body of the dress and a diamond pattern for the two borders, which are seven inches wide at top and bottom. These borders must both be completed before the center is begun, because of the complicated heddle setup required for the diamond weave. One border is finished and then the entire loom is inverted for the completion of the second border. Subsequently, the diagonal pattern is set up with a new heddle division and the weaving continues upward toward the first border.[40] The center section differs from the borders not only in weave, but often also in color; for instance, a black center may have dark blue borders, or a brown center may have black borders.

These blankets may be used as shawls and mantles as well as dresses. To fashion one into a dress, it is wrapped about the body and joined with red yarn part way up on the right side. The upper edges are drawn over the right shoulder and fastened there, leaving an opening for the right arm with the ends forming a kind of sleeve. The left arm and shoulder are bare and free. The break between the border and the center is often covered by cording or stitching of red and green yarn (pl. 19).

The Hopi men weave these blankets, which are in great demand among all the pueblos. In each village the inhabitants decorate the borders and sew the dresses in their own way. The Zuñi use a strong, embroidered border in dark blue. At Acoma, Tesuque, and Laguna red and green yarns have been introduced.

On rare occasions is seen a dark dress made of two pieces of cloth sewn up each side.[41] It is worn in the same manner as the one-piece dark dress. It is obvious that the smaller pieces of cloth would require a correspondingly small loom for the weaving.

In these native homespun woolen blanket dresses we see one of the last stands of the native culture. No matter how decadent and Americanized a village has become, it is still possible to find one of these original dresses

PLATE 19. *Simple costume for women. Tablita Dance, Santo Domingo.*   ⟫⟫→

Plate 19

on some old grandmother puttering about her daily work, or on some actor performing in a dance which has its roots deep in native custom.

There is a special white ceremonial dress (pl. 22). It is woven of cotton, a plain weave, and decorated with wide bands of colored embroidery at top and bottom. So is the white mantle. The two garments are often interchangeable, although there is supposed to be an appreciable difference in size. The mantle originated from the great white robe and the dress from the smaller robe, both of which were woven for each Hopi bride at the time of her marriage. Today there are worn under these dresses other dresses of manufactured cloth with long sleeves and high necklines and trimmed with lace and fancy braid. The impersonators of female characters have sometimes taken over this added garment, as in the Kokochi ceremony at Zuñi.

Trousers.—During the period of Spanish settlement and influence, a kind of trousers became a part of the men's everyday dress. Its origin is uncertain. It could have come with the colonists from Spain by way of Mexico and it could have developed from the hip-length leggings made of animal skin. In any event, there appeared loose white cotton trousers, of about ankle length, made of two straight pieces of material seamed on the outside of the leg. These trousers were gathered on a cord about the waist, the top was concealed under the long tails of the shirt, and the breechclout protected the opening. A slit from the bottom almost to the knee was made on the outside of each leg.[42] Similar hip-length leggings of skin and colored flannel are found among the Rio Grande Pueblos. At Taos today, by a ruling of their council of governors, a man is not permitted to wear modern trousers.[43] As a compromise, the seat is removed and the breechclout substituted.

Trousers are not often worn in the ceremonial dances. One may, however, see them on members of the choir, the standard bearer, those who impersonate hunters, and a few supernaturals (for example, the Nataka men, pl. 33).

LEG COVERINGS

Leggings.—In the northern Rio Grande pueblos knitted or crocheted leggings of white cotton cord are often worn by dancers today (pl. 27). They may be fringed on the outside or up the front with cotton cord, and by various groupings of stitches patterns are worked into the body of the garments. Some of these leggings appear to cover the knee; others are only of knee length and are held in place by woven garters. A knee-length knitted legging of dark wool is also found in nearly all the villages. At Zuñi the leaders who are priests, and the impersonators of the female deities, often wear them (pl. 38). Investigators who visited the pueblos in the latter part of the nineteenth century saw them on both old men and old women as part of the everyday dress in cold weather." As a protective garment, red-brown deerskin leggings (pl. 33) were worn above the moccasins by men. Each one was made of a single piece of tanned skin wrapped about the leg and secured by a woven garter tied just below the knee. They may be seen today in the western pueblos.[45]

Garters.—Woven garters are made on a loom similar to the one used for belts. With a tapestry weave, vertical strips and small geometric designs are made in red, green, and white or black yarn. The garters are wrapped twice around the leg and tied at the front or side. When worn with the slit trouser leg, the ends show at the opening. They are used simply to hold the leggings in place or as a decorative motif at the knees of the dancers, whose legs are otherwise bare or painted. Strands of yarn—red, dark blue, or black—are also used as garters or leg bands. They are knotted so that the long ends swing free about the legs (pl. 20).

Anklets.—Anklets, worn on the lower leg, are of leather or small sprigs of evergreen (pl. 6) bound together in a festoon. The leather bands are stained a solid color or striped with various pigments; or a rectangular piece of leather is slit into internal strips which may be wound with colored yarns, or with porcupine quills and horsehair in geometric patterns.

All these forms may be worn when the feet are bare, or the leather bands and the slit and wound anklets may make the heelpieces of moccasins.

Moccasins.—Moccasins are made with hard soles and soft deerskin uppers. The soles are cut from rawhide or the tanned, thick, neckskin of the deer, which is exceptionally strong and heavy. These soles, after shaping

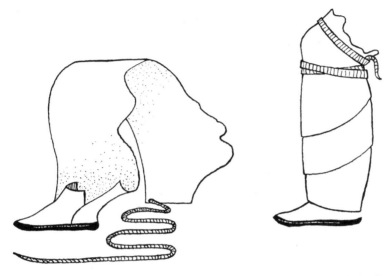

FIGURE 17. Woman's wrapped moccasin of white deerskin with polished black sole.

and puckering, come well up at toe and sides. The man's brown moccasin is usually made from a one-piece upper which overlaps at the outside of the leg. It is tied with thongs or buttoned with small silver conchs of Navaho workmanship. This moccasin is high, reaching several inches above the ankle (pl. 35). Another type has a two-piece upper (pl. 8), one piece being sewn to the sole from instep to instep around the toe, covering the front of the foot and making a tongue. The second piece is sewn around the heel and then wrapped about the ankle. This piece also overlaps on the outside of the foot and is tied with two or three thongs. The top is turned down to make a cuff with the longer tab outside, concealing the opening. To add a decorative touch an extra flap may be sewn in front to the lower edge of this wrapped piece.

The special Hopi and Zuñi dance moccasin is made in this latter pattern, with turquoise blue paint covering the body of the footgear, the cuff and added piece in front being stained red or yellow.[46] The sole is painted black and highly polished. Among the Rio Grande Pueblos the ceremonial moccasins are whitened with kaolin, which makes a strong contrast with the shiny black soles (pl. 20). Occasionally, lower moccasins are worn. These fit snugly and barely cover the ankle (pl. 25). They are sometimes beaded, and are obtained by purchase from the Plains tribes.

In ceremonial dress, heelpieces are worn with the moccasins. At Hopi a fringed piece of red-brown deerskin is secured around the ankle. It is worn by dancing Kachinas as well as the Snake Priests, whose entire costume is blended harmoniously with the red-brown skin. Solid, rectangular pieces of leather; or pieces slit and wound with different-colored yarns, or porcupine quills and horsehair; or strips of buffalo, bear, or skunk fur—all are tied about the ankle and knotted over the instep with one or two thongs. The skunk fur is said to keep the evil spirits from entering the body of the dancer by way of the earth, and it is the only part of a dancer's costume which symbolizes death.[47]

Patterned like the two-piece footgear of the men, the women's moccasins are white with black soles. They have a high ankle flap, very long because it consists of a whole, white, tanned deerskin.[48] This is wrapped many times, spirally, about the leg and ends well above the knee, and is held in place by a well-tied thong of buckskin. The many folds give these moccasins a clumsy look, but they make the feet appear very small and dainty.[49] The size of the moccasin leg indicates the wealth of the Pueblo woman. The deerskin is whitened with a wash of kaolin which approximates our white shoe cleaner. It is considered fashionable, among the Keres and the Tewa, to stain the toes of these moccasins pink or red.[50]

At Taos, and frequently among the Tewa, one other form of woman's moccasin is seen. It is a kind of boot with a hard black sole and an upper

---

PLATE 20. *Men's simple costume. Tablita Dance, Santo Domingo.*   >>>→

Plate 20

made of two pieces of deerskin sewed together with seams on each side. The top comes up very wide from the ankle, and from the side gives an appearance of flatness. The width depends upon the size of the skins and the wealth of the individual who purchases them. There are from two to five pleats of the skin above the ankle, around which is a drawstring of

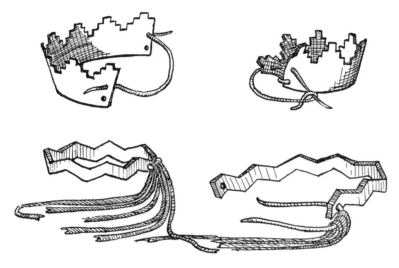

FIGURE 18. Leather arm bands.

deerskin.[51] As the soles wear through, a pleat is loosened and the top pulled down to sew on the new soles. A pair of moccasins made for a woman at the time of her marriage will last her the rest of her life.

ARM ORNAMENTS

Arm bands.—Because of his love of ornament the Indian wears above his elbow decorative bands in which he can place pieces of evergreen or tie soft, bright feathers or tassels of yarn. These ornaments represent the sacred butterfly, a love charm which is supposed to have the power to make people crazy.[52] They may be merely strips of leather, striped or painted a solid color, and some are cut with dentate edges. They are tied together with thongs or tassels of yarn. Arm bands are also made of the hair of buffalo or goat to conform in color and spirit with the other details of the costume (pls. 21, 22). The goat's hair is often dyed.

Strands of colored yarns are used to decorate the wrists. Wrist guards are worn on the left arm during the Hunt Dances, because originally this guard was a leather band worn to protect the wrist from the sharp impact of the bowstring when an arrow was released from the bow. Since the introduction of silver, a curved plate, often set with turquoise, has been applied to the upper side of this decoration.[53]

ACCESSORIES

Sash.—A brocade sash (pl. 31) is worn by the men who take part in public ceremonies. Each sash is made up of two "panels of plain weaving of cotton or wool, decorated at the end with designs in colored yarns and terminating with a fringe."[54] Two-thirds of each panel is plain-woven; then the heddles of the loom are adjusted to work the pattern in yarn. At the point where this decoration begins, a finer weft is used so that the addition of the colored yarns does not widen the cloth. The designs are virtually alike, being made up of bands of black, green, and blue with a red diamond design in the center. At their plain ends the two panels are sewn together with a roving of cord. This produces a long sash which can be wrapped about the waist and knotted on the right side with the ends hanging to the calf of the leg. The origin of the sash appears to be unknown, but the form was fully developed in the earliest modern examples collected by James Stevenson in 1879.[55] The sashes are brocaded today with commercial yarns; "however, old specimens show hand-spun wool for both the body of the sash and the brocading."[56]

The plaited white cotton sash with its long fringe is one of the most significant and potent of rainmaking garments. "A typical example of the sacred sash is composed of 216 threads of white cotton about the size of small package cord braided into a band eight inches wide and sixty-one

PLATE 21. *Animal impersonation. Buffalo Dance, San Ildefonso.*　　　》》》→

Plate 21

inches long to the termination of the solid braiding. The work is started midway of the cords when a twining is applied temporarily, and proceeds toward either end when the cords are divided into twelve tresses braided into narrow tapes for a short distance."[57] Over each tape end, rings of corn-husk wrapped with cotton cord are slipped and tied in place. The cords are then divided into sixes and twisted together to form a long fringe, which symbolizes, in the Indian mind, the falling of the rain in its long, parallel lines (pl. 20). These sashes are kept clean and white by rubbing with liquid kaolin.

Belt.—The woven belt, ordinarily worn by the women around their everyday dresses of dark wool, became a part of the ceremonial costume because of its usefulness and its striking colors. Walter Hough remarks that "the greatest play of fancy in the Hopi textile art is the weaving of belts."[58] In this article of apparel there could be produced small and greatly varied patterns not limited by ceremonial rules (fig. 10, p. 58). Woven on an easily manipulated small loom, warp threads to form the designs could be picked out by hand. "The warp and weft are often of the same yarn, giving uniformity of texture, but usually the warp is partly of yarn of the same thickness as the weft yarn and partly smaller. This arrangement furnishes a fertile field for the play of design. The warp in the central or pattern band of a belt is generally of small white yarn and another color of larger yarn, usually red, the former working out white pattern grounds, having raised figures in red warp, the latter contrast being produced by the difference in size of the yarns, the small warp being worked singly and the larger in pairs."[59] The use of small and large warps gives an uneven surface to the material and is the only example in Pueblo weaving in which this method of obtaining variety is found. The most prevalent color scheme is composed of a wide center of red broken by black designs and edged with two stripes of green which in turn are bordered by two narrow lines of black. Other combinations show a red center with white designs, a black and red stripe, and a final line of white on each side; or a red center with white patterns, a stripe of blue-green, one of ultramarine followed by one of red, and a final edging of white. The patterns are manifold geometric forms made up of small triangles and with lines repeated in different and varying combinations.

The women wear this belt wrapped several times around the waist, drawn in tightly, with part of the loose fringe tucked under a lap so that the rest falls down on the left side. The brilliant color of the belt is a conspicuous accent on the dark garment (pl. 1). The width varies from three to five inches and the tight wrapping helps to confine the figure. The men dancers use this belt to hold their kilts in place or to encircle their bodies over the brocaded sash. When worn in the latter fashion, one part is looped over and the fringe of the two ends hangs to the middle of the calf of the leg. In the Peace Dance of the Tewa, which depicts a combat between chiefs of opposing forces, "a description of the battle which brought peace to the tribe,"[60] the wife of each chief appears holding one end of a belt which is fastened to her husband's waist. The significance of this is that behind all warfare the ties of family and home life are vital incentives to valorous deeds.[61]

Foxskin.—A noticeable feature of many of the costumes is the pendent foxskin, worn tail downward at the back of the belt (pls. 24, 35). This particular fox, formerly indigenous to the mountainous country of the Pueblos, is a small animal with gray hair intermingled with amber. It was hunted during the season of the year when the hair was long and thick and the hide tough. When killed, the body of the animal was skinned very carefully and all the parts were retained: the paws remained on the legs, and the ears were kept on the full head covering. Ruth Bunzel says that the foxskin tail is "considered as a relic of the earliest days of man, for the katcinas were transformed while mankind was still tailed and horned."[62] For several days previous to each occasion on which they are worn, the pelts are buried in damp sand in order to bring suppleness to

PLATE 22. *Women's costume. Buffalo Dance, San Ildefonso.*   )))→

Plate 22

the skin and a soft, live quality to the fur. In most of the ceremonies the men dancers wear foxskins. This custom evidently carries for the Rio Grande Pueblos no association with animal tails, for none of their hunt impersonators wear them, but, instead, affect the fringes of the plaited sash (pl. 26) or a fan of eagle feathers (pl. 23) on the belt at the rear. The Hopi and Zuñi animal impersonators wear pendent foxskins, but not as animal tails; their use by these performers conforms entirely to the conventional kachina dress.

Bandoleers.—Many kinds of bandoleers are worn over the right shoulder, and at the same time they encircle the body to the waist on the left side. The more common and concededly less potent kinds are broad bands of ribbon,[63] beadwork from the plains, red woven belts,[64] twists of yucca cord or leather and cedar berries. Conch shells (*Conus*) strung on thongs or yucca cord are highly prized for their rarity.[65] "Warrior katcinas wear the bandoleer of the bow priest over their right shoulder. This is made of white buckskin, decorated with fringes under the left arm and ornamented with a zigzag pattern of shells, four for each scalp taken. A little of the hair from each scalp is sewed into the broad fringed portion. The bandoleers of the bow priests hang by outer doors of their houses. They are never taken into back rooms. They must always be removed before going into the room with the corn, or before drinking, lest the spring from which the water was drawn be contaminated.* The bandoleers of the bow priests may be borrowed or imitated."[66] Double bandoleers are also worn, hanging from each shoulder and crossing on the chest and back.[67] Impersonators concerned with the hunt often have pouches suspended, like the bandoleer, from the right shoulder (pl. 5). They are similar to those which "hunters use to carry their animal fetishes and prayer meal."[68]

Jewelry.—Above all else among his purely private and individual possessions, the Pueblo Indian prizes his jewelry. Apparently he has done so

---

* The enemy are supposed to be very dangerous and often are witches who weave magical spells.

from the earliest time. Archaeologists have unearthed many smoothly turned disks of stone and shell pierced with a hole in the center for the purpose of being strung on thongs of deerskin. Furthermore, great numbers of crude beads and pendants have been found, which undoubtedly were worn as necklaces and earbobs by the prehistoric men who lived in cliff houses and communal towns.

The Indian first used as jewelry whatever was near at hand of a decorative nature. Seed pods, acorn hulls,[69] the teeth and bones of animals picked up promiscuously and perforated and strung together to be hung about his person—these were the early and crude expression of this intimate kind of ornamentation. As his culture evolved, his amazing capacity for painstaking labor developed new forms of beads from the more precious materials. Soon he was not only adorning himself with the gray-white sea shells obtained from the far Pacific or from the scintillating waters of the Gulf, and with the reddish coral brought back by runners from their trading expeditions into Mexico, but was also decking his neck and arms and ears with ornaments made of the brilliant turquoise with its matrix of soft brown. This was mined from the rough stretches to the east of the Rio Grande and to the south of Zuñi. Beads were also made from the chunks of lignite and the dull pink quartz which crumbled from the outcroppings along the rocky ridges.

Many kinds of shells were used as bead and ornament. The small, barrel-shaped olive shell (*Olivella*) with its tapering ends and the tiny conch with its reducing spiral could be strung together one after the other on necklace or bandoleer, or tied to buckskin and fabric as tinkler and fringe. Multitudinous flat shells, either whole or in part, were brought into use as bead and pendant. The larger, oval abalone shell (*Haliotis*) was often hung at the base of the neck, where its iridescent, pearly inner surface gleamed softly against the rich brown tones of the skin (pl. 21).

With its piercing blue, the turquoise reflects the power and glory of the daytime sky from which come life and beauty in the warmth of the purifying and nurturing sun and the repose of the rain-bringing and shadowing cloud. Turquoise is the most highly prized of the Indian gems, and it has been worn throughout the entire historic period of Pueblo life; in the records of the Coronado expedition it was noted that the Pueblo Indians wore turquoise in their ears "as well as on their necks and on their wrists."[70] Moreover, it has value as an economic investment. At Zuñi, "after the sale of wool in the spring a man liquidates his debts and invests the balance in turquoise."[71]

The bright, soft red of the coral is used to offset and intensify the beauty of the turquoise. Thus the Indian is able to combine two natural elements which complement each other in color and equal each other in tone value.

Since the earliest times, small disk-shaped beads have been made by the Pueblos. In excavations and ruins many examples of exquisite workmanship have been found. The process by which these beads are now made is as follows. The material is roughly chipped out to a little more than the desired size, and then a hole is

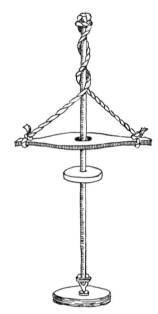

FIGURE 19. Rotary drill.

bored in the center with a drill pump. This is a device like the spindle, with a flywheel on a long, slender shaft. A stone or metal point is attached to one end, and at the other two buckskin thongs support a crosspiece with a large hole in which the shaft may move freely. The buckskin thongs are twisted around the shaft, and the point of the drill is placed in the center of the bead and made to revolve by a pumping motion with the crosspiece, while the flywheel produces rotation which unwinds the thongs in one direction and rewinds them in the other. The bead is drilled halfway through from one side and then is turned over and the drilling is completed. Shell beads require but few strokes, whereas turquoise, jet, and coral require much drilling. When a number of rough beads have been drilled, they are strung in a tight column on a length of cord and the whole string is ground to an even size on a slab of sandstone or between two stones.[72] The beads are then sorted and matched by color and size, and strung in necklaces of one, two, or even four strands. White shell is often interspersed with small symmetrical beads or large, rough chunks of turquoise, and short strings of turquoise with a few beads of coral are looped over the long strands and bunched together at the bottom. These same small strings of turquoise are sometimes tied with thongs in the ears and from this position peep from beneath the black, bobbed side hair.

Another form of jewellike decoration is the mosaic pendant, delicate and of beautiful design. Mosaics consist mainly of small, flat pieces of turquoise, coral, quartz, and jet set together in simple patterns. Their base is the softly curving back of a clamlike shell or a glittering piece of jet, to which they are glued with piñon gum.

When the Spanish colonists came, silver was introduced to the pueblos. For a long time this new material had little or no effect on the Indian, and then suddenly there sprang up a remarkable silver-working industry. This was dominated by the Navaho.[73] Today the foremost jewelers among the pueblos are the people of Zuñi and Santo Domingo. Here, round silver beads, and occasionally the conventionalized silver squash blossoms, are strung into necklaces terminating, like those of the Navaho, in a curved pendant set with turquoise. Turquoise and the soft, rich silver are used together in a hundred patterns. "The Zuñis are freest in combining these two elements; with them a silver bracelet is hardly more than a setting for fine, deep blue stones."[74]

Silver earrings are shaped to resemble the dragonfly, the butterfly, or some bird, and all are set with turquoise. Silver and turquoise rings are ubiquitous, as jewelry is worn by all: men, women, and children. Proud is the mother whose baby wears about his neck a string of tiny turquoise

PLATE 23. *Realism in bird impersonation. Eagle Dance, Rio Grande.* ⟫→

Plate 23

beads, or on his arm a little silver bracelet. "The amount of turquoise worn by an impersonator is limited only by his borrowing capacity. The necklaces cover the whole chest, frequently also the whole back. . . . The way of wearing the necklaces is indicative of rank and position. Necklaces front and back indicate a Katcina of importance; necklaces doubled over and worn close to the throat are a badge of society membership."[75]

Sun-disk ornament.—A disk surrounded by feathers is the most prominently used of the separate ornaments. It symbolizes the sun and often has stylized features painted on its buckskin face. Sometimes the disk is a round bunch of gaily colored feathers, and the diverging rays are reduced to a few long shafts of brilliant colors across the top (pl. 22); at others, the entire circumference is decked with the severe black and white of the eagle wing feathers shot through with long, waving strands of red horsehair.

A similar disk is fastened to the end of a pole and used in kiva rituals when the ceremony has to do with the sun. It is raised, lowered, or twirled as the action in the rite demands.[76]

DANCE PROPERTIES

Rattles.—Rattles accompany every Pueblo dance. Frequently they are incorporated as decorative elements on separate garments, as, for example, the shell, hoof, and cone tinklers on the kilt and the legging fringes. Nowadays, American-made sleighbells are seen on straps around the knees and arms and on belts around the waist.

Perhaps the most interesting rattle is that of tortoise shell (pl. 20) worn by almost every masked dancer. It is a rattle of especial sacredness because the tortoise lives in the water and has influence with the Rain Gods. When the men wear tortoise shell in the dance, the belief is that the supernaturals hear the rattle and thus know that the Indian needs rain for his crops. The tortoise is captured near the water holes or sacred springs. After the shells are cleaned and dried, the toes of deer are tied on by a piece of buckskin rove through holes in one side of the shell. A second piece of thong, passed through holes in the other side, ties the shell around the leg just under the knee. As the foot is lifted in the dance, the leg hits the pendent hoofs, sending them up to strike the back of the shell with a loud, sharp clatter.*

Shells and the dewclaws of various animals are hung on thongs and fastened to little sticks so that they produce a clicking noise. The gourd rattles are the ones most frequently carried. The dried shell of the gourd is thoroughly cleaned; then the seeds are removed through a small hole and replaced by pebbles of white quartz, colored stone, or small crystals.⁷ When the gourd has no neck by which the rattle may be carried, a corn-cob or wooden handle is in-

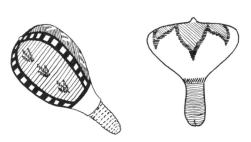

FIGURE 20. Gourd rattles.

serted in the hole. Occasionally, a tapering handle goes all the way through the gourd and is held in place by a peg on the other side. These rattles are painted in divers colors and in designs appropriate to the suggestion of motion.

Skin rattles are made of pieces of rawhide sewn together in rectangular or ring shapes. Pebbles are enclosed and a handle is affixed. A special Antelope-fraternity rattle at Hopi is made of a dampened skin stretched over a wooden hoop perpendicular to a wooden handle, the whole forming a kind of frame. The skin is pulled completely around this frame, the rattle is put in, and the skin is fastened and painted white. The sound of this rattle is similar to the warning of the rattlesnake, a rattle with a rustling quality rather than the loud sharpness of the gourd.

Before it is carried in a ceremony, each rattle is 'blessed' by tying on it with cotton cord a downy white eagle or 'breath' feather. At the top

* At Isleta a distinction is made: shells of the water turtle are worn by one group, and those of the land turtle by another (Parsons, 1932, p. 355).

of the long standard carried by the leader of the chorus there are a decorated gourd rattle and many feathers, as well as the swirling white kilt
or banner. Bunches of horns from cow and mountain sheep may be carried noisily about by the Rain Makers, while hoofs of cattle, shoulder
blades of sheep, and bones of other animals serve the purpose of rattles
and noisemakers. A thin, rhomboidal piece of wood tied to the end of
a string or thong is whirled rapidly through the air like a bull-roarer and

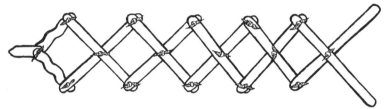

FIGURE 21. Lazy tongs lightning frame.

adds its appreciable measure of noise (pl. 40). In the ceremonial dance
it is often handled by one of the clown priests.

Wands.—The priest leaders carry several different feather wands. These
are the insignia of the kiva or organization which happens to be performing. Moreover, these brilliantly clothed fetishes are works of art by reason
of the careful selection and arrangement of feathers and the remarkable
precision with which each feather is bound in place.

There is a lightning wand which is cut from wood in a zigzag shape to
imitate that phenomenon of nature. It is carried by certain impersonators
in dances devoted to rainmaking.[78] The quick striking of the lightning
is represented to the Indian mind by a mechanized frame of strips of
wood, pegged or tied together like a lazy tongs, folded and unfolded by
two handles at one end.[79] This is one of their most highly developed mechanical devices, and the ceremonial lightning thus created never fails
to inspire the spectators with wonder and amazement. Representations
of lightning end in arrow-shaped points because the Pueblo Indian believes that each flash is tipped with a stone knife.[80]

Warriors and those concerned with the hunt always carry brightly painted, curved rabbit sticks or bows and arrows trimmed with downy eagle feathers which float from the tips and interspacings along the strings. Sprigs of evergreen are carried in the hand, parallel to the bow.

At Santa Clara a section of gourd is mounted on a short stick and carried by each male dancer in the Zuñi Basket Dance. This piece of gourd is painted green on the concave surface and decorated with four eagle feathers. It is said to represent the sun, especially when stick and emblem are held aloft.[81]

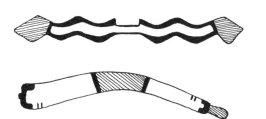

FIGURE 22. Hopi dance wands: upper, lightning dance wand; lower, rabbit-stick dance wand.

The women's dance wands are rectangular tablets with a handle at one end. In dancing for rain these are carried vertically in each hand. A single, wide tablet may have two handles side by side; it is then carried with both hands in front of the body.[82] In the center is painted a figure of a rain god with curving cloud shapes and streaks of rain above him and a stylized ear of corn below. The whole is topped with downy feathers and crisp yellow heads of seed grass, and puffs of eagle down float at intervals from each side. At Zuñi another hand wand, of great beauty, is carried. It is made of slender sticks "about eighteen inches long, painted white and adorned with delicate white duck feathers in groups of two, the space between being the width of the first three fingers placed crosswise within a few inches of their ends."[83] There are also little, formal bouquets made of feathers beautifully arranged with respect to color and size, and having borders of evergreens and a final edging of shells or dainty, bone-colored dewclaws of the deer or antelope (pl. 22).

Many of the dancers carry tall staffs to indicate their office or to give

PLATE 24. *Eagle Kachina, Hopi. Bird form stylized by introduction of all the elements of the conventional kachina costume.*   》》》→

Plate 24

dignity to their impersonations (pls. 29, 30). The staffs are variously ornamented with feathers, evergreen, cornhusks, ears of corn, and other
sacred symbols.

Baskets.—The round, flat, basket plaques, made by the Hopi or purchased by other villages from nomadic neighbors, are used most signifi-
cantly in the Basket Dance. This is definitely a
woman's dance, though sometimes the services of a
few men are utilized. The major symbolism is centered in the food basket, the usefulness of which is
inestimable since it covers the span of life. It holds
all the seeds to be planted in the earth, in due time
to flower and become grain. It carries the ripened
harvest and winnows the seed from the chaff. When
the harvest is ground, it bears the meal, and later it
brings the thin, colored rolls of piki bread which is
made for the sustenance and ceremony of the tribe.[84]

FIGURE 23. Zuñi dance
wand carried by women
dancers. Designs repre-
sent cloud, rain god,
and corn.

The Hopi baskets are made with both the coil
and the wicker technique. They are constructed of
the tough, strong stems and small twigs of various
desert plants which have been cleaned and dyed the
pleasing soft colors of earth and herb. The two techniques are very different. The wicker designs diverge as they leave the
center, growing larger and more effective, whereas the coilwork restricts
the design to a radial pattern which is forced out from center to circumference and has a tighter and more concentrated feeling. Baskets are made
specially for this ceremony and at the end of the dance are thrown to the
onlookers, to the accompaniment of clamor and agitation.

In the Sun Basket Dance of Santa Clara, performed by two boys and
two girls, each of the girls "carries a basket decorated inside with an
orange-colored sun symbol and on the edge with long fringes of red-dyed
angora wool. In the principal movement of the dance these baskets are

swung in a double arc, with graceful drooping of the entire body, the flame-colored corona flashing out in a conventionalized but quite realistic picture of the sun."[85]

A greater number of symbolic elements are to be found among the objects carried in the hands of dancers and impersonators than in the colors and designs of dress and mask. With their background in literal fact and phenomena, these objects have outgrown their material phase and have become ceremonial. Devices making use of mechanics in construction are here displayed in their most advanced form. The Pueblo Indian has never been mechanically gifted; even today he has an utter lack of knowledge and interest in the mechanistic features of civilization; his most advanced development in this direction is gauged by his childish delight and wondering belief in the reality of the serpent effigy and its simple manipulation by stick or horsehair thread. His talent lies in another field. By neglecting the mechanical forms he has advanced in the art of surface decoration. He has gained mastery in the field of design.

MAKE-UP

There are two modes of approach to the decoration of the face for the ceremonial dances. On the one hand, the Indian used the patterns of the body paint, continuing the color and designs up over the face and into and over the hair. The "Chiffoneti" is a striking example. His black and white striped body is topped with a neck, face, and exaggerated hairdress which are also striped and circled in black and white (pl. 39). On the other hand, the Indian treated the face as a separate and distinct element of the figure and provided for it a make-up which, like the mask, characterized the impersonation. In neither mode was there any attempt at realism, even in the animal forms. The colors and patterns of make-up depend, like the body paint, not only upon the impersonation, but also

---

PLATE 25. *Deer dancer, Taos. The simplest and most realistic form of animal impersonation.*   ⟫→

Plate 25

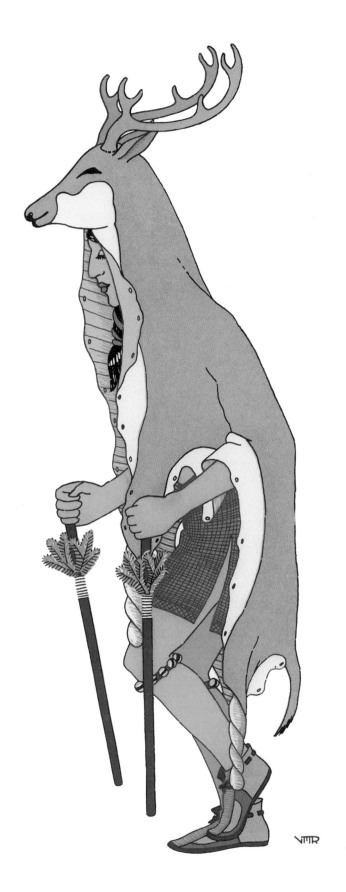

upon the pueblo and the society or group which is performing. The Deer Dancers at San Ildefonso paint their faces black with a white rim around the edge (pl. 26). At San Juan the same group paint the face red with no relief trimming (pl. 27).

Face paint may well have originated from the application of a coating of earth to the face in order to protect it from the elements. At Taos today, "red paint is smeared on the faces of the men in very cold weather, against the wind."[86] However, there is hardly a rite from which make-up is omitted. The simplest form of it is found in the brilliant carmine dots which accent the faces of the men and women in the Hopi Butterfly Dance.

The face may be painted a solid color. Occasionally, streaks of another hue may be added under the eyes. Sometimes each side is painted a different color and the division is a vertical line in the exact middle of the face. Racers at Cochiti are painted thus, one side of the face red and the other green.[87] Sometimes the face is divided horizontally. Hopi Snake Dancers are painted black to the mouth and white to the neck. Often other and more brilliant colors are used.

When carefully applied, the paint practically conceals the identity of the impersonator. Dancers often wear make-up under their masks so that they will not be recognized by the children if by chance they are caught without their masks during the rest periods. At Zuñi the face paint under the mask consists of two lines drawn across the face in iridescent black paint or red pigment, or it consists of red or black dots on cheeks and chin.[88] There is never any attempt to delineate human features, as the paint is used for concealment and ceremonial significance. The color and pigment are applied in stipulated patterns to satisfy the occasion.

HEADDRESSES

The true marks of identification in ceremonial costumes are found in the headdresses. The hair is generally permitted to float free. From the banged forelocks to the bobbed side hair and thence to the long back strands there is recognizable the geometric stepped form so often associated by the Indian with cloud terraces. Impersonators whose hair has been cut wear wigs of long horsehair. Certain actors who are impersonating comic characters wear short wigs of different kinds of hair and wool. There are also fringes and bangs of horsehair, goat's hair, and sheep's wool which are tied across the forehead or worn all the way around the head. Sometimes the hair is worn in a wrapped club at the neck or wound into whorls or tied with yarn over wooden frames (pl. 38).

Every performer wears some ornament in his hair, even if it is no more than the white, downy, "breath" feather or a red, downy badge of office. Sometimes the green or yellow pompon of gleaming parrot feathers (pl. 20), from its place on top of the head, moves in accordance with the dancer's steps. More elaborate ornaments of feathers and carved gourd are worn from side to side or from front to back.

The narrow bandeau of deerskin, or fillet of yucca leaves, may be worn alone on the head or it may serve as a base for other ornamentation. Flower symbols of gourd or cornhusks, painted in simple colors, can be fastened at the side or front, and elaborate forms made of little sticks set at angles to a small round piece of wood are twined with colored yarns to represent a squash blossom, from the center of which floats a gently swaying downy feather (pl. 9). Buffalo or cow horns, or imitations of these made from long gourd necks, are fastened to one or both sides.

The war bonnet, generally associated with the fiercer Indian tribes, has its counterpart in the Pueblo dress. It is made with the buckskin cap base or the simple bandeau, in which feathers are stuck upright around the head and down the two side streamers. In contrast to more generally recognized forms, these streamers reach to just below the shoulders, and in all probability are influenced by the attire which has been borrowed or purchased from other tribes. The simple roach of tall feathers stands upright from the forelock across the crown and ends in a long streamer floating to the middle of the back. This is popular in many villages.

The basic form of the women's headdresses is a strip of deerskin crossing the crown of the head from ear to ear and secured beneath the chin. Ornaments may be applied at the top and sides (fig. 13, p. 83). A common headdress is the tablet, or flat upright plaque of wood, or the wooden frame covered with deerskin or cloth. The simplest form is found among the Rio Grande pueblos, where a rectangular tablet (pl. 19), terraced at the top and with incisions in the center, is worn across the head and held in place by a band or thong tied under the chin. This form is prevalent throughout the Pueblo span and its shape and elaboration appear to develop, as has been noted of the mask, as one goes westward.

FIGURE 24. Wooden head tablet worn by women, showing pad which protects the head.

At Zuñi, a thin board terraced at the top is perched upright on a caplike base made of strips of deerskin sewn on one end to the bandeau and attached together at the crown of the head (pl. 10). This is worn by the Corn Maidens when they return to the village in their special ceremony, a ritual which originally took place every four years. This slender form is decorated with symbols of the sun, moon, and stars, and at the terraced top are two downy feathers. Small, geometric wooden forms of the various directional colors are set on the bandeau where the cross strips intersect.[89] In the Butterfly Dance of the Hopi, a dance performed by the Butterfly Clan,[90] who are said to have been prehistoric colonists from the Rio Grande pueblos,[91] a tablet similar to those of the east is worn by the women. However, among the Hopi the form is often elaborated, as it is made of many separate shapes each suggesting some symbolic form. These shapes are put together by means of pegs and buckskin thongs until they are built up to a mass which assumes very large proportions. The most familiar design elements employed are clouds, butterflies, sprouting corn, and rain, and the bright colors are sharply contrasted. Black is frequently used to outline the separate shapes and to accent the divisions of various patterns.

Another common headdress is one which completely covers the top of the head. This is used mainly in dances requiring more elaborate impersonations. It may likewise be made on a base of deerskin with the decorative incorporation of horns, flowers, and feathers.

Closest to the mask forms, but without actually concealing the wearer, are the animal headdresses of the Rio Grande pueblos. They vary from the simple deerskin cap to which the horns have been applied, to the actual animal head (pl. 25) cured and with the horns intact. When the horn-ornamented deerskin cap is used, the long space from the neck to the waist is filled with sheaves of various feathers which are laid in series and accented with dotlike puffs of down (pl. 26).

MASKS

The mask is the most individualizing and most highly developed article worn by the Pueblo actors in their prayer dramas. Through the various combinations of shapes, colors, and decorations used to distinguish one character from another, unlimited characterizations are possible.

The Indian believes that the spirit of the supernatural whom he portrays is incorporate in the mask which he wears, and that he takes on the personality of the god by assuming the god's mask. "The mask is one of the variable features that arise out of the spirit-traffic of primitive man. It is a sort of animated fetish through which he works magic and controls the spirits."[92] The Pueblo Indian dons the mask and becomes the transubstantiated kachina. He then proceeds, through the medium of the song and the dance, to offer prayers to the all-powerful spirits, entreating them to come to his aid. It is necessary that the mask conceal the identity of the

PLATE 26. *Deer dancer, San Ildefonso. A step toward stylization; the impersonator has put on conventional ceremonial dress.* 〉〉〉→

Plate 26

actual person because that person is no longer believed to exist after
assuming the personality of the god.

It cannot be learned whether the first mask was a strip worn over the
face or a bag worn over the head. These two mask types may have originated simultaneously. It is a fact that at Zuñi the Kokochi, who is said
to be the prototype of the earliest kachina, wears a half mask which
consists of a simple strip of leather across the face (pl. 37). The myths
say that he is the first-born of the "old dance woman," the mother of the
kachina. Her husband and her other nine sons become the Mudheads,[93]
who are distinguished by their baglike masks of cotton cloth (pl. 40).
Thus the contemporary affinity between the strip mask and the bag mask
is established.

Half mask.—We may begin, then, with the simple strip of leather, the
half mask (pl. 11). It is deep enough to cover the face from hairline to
mouth, and it reaches across the face from ear to ear. It was doubtless
intended to conceal the features only, leaving the bangs and side hair
of the wearer to cover the edges. Half masks seen today are made of pieces
of heavy buckskin or rawhide, secured by thongs passing over and around
the head. There are small slits for the eyes, and, around these, eye designs
are painted with little regard to conformity with the slits. A bang is made
across the upper edge with a thick fringe of horsehair or goat's hair. Across
the lower edge is a strip of leather about two inches wide. Sometimes
it is painted in blocks of black and white or in various colors, symbolizing clouds. From the under side hangs a long beard of shiny black horsehair which covers the mouth and chin of the wearer[94] and eliminates the
need of a hole for breathing. This form of mask permits a dancer's voice
to be heard clearly when he accompanies his movement with song. The
removable beard is made of long strands of horsehair held in place by
three cotton strings which are braided together between each strand or
sewn to a strip of cloth. The beard can be tied in place by deerskin thongs
provided on the inside of the leather half mask. Sometimes the smooth

black surface of the beard is broken by white downy eagle feathers hung from the lower edge of the mask by white cotton cords. The horsehair may be replaced by numerous small bunches of the tail feathers of many little birds. These feathers form a fringe about five inches deep across the bottom of the mask.[95] It splays out at the bottom and shows feathers of many colors as each bunch rises and falls with the movements of the dancer. In the center, hanging on longer cords beneath the fringe, are four or five additional bunches of feathers interspersed with white downy eagle feathers.

These half masks are often worn by female deities (pl. 38). The design on the lower borders, and the color, either white or yellow, distinguish the wearers from the male deities, who wear blue half masks.

Face mask.—From this half mask to the face mask (pl. 12) was only a step. The simple strip of leather grew longer and was drawn under the chin with another and triangular piece of leather sewn into the gap. This mask, still depending upon the bangs and side hair of the wearer, has evolved into forms which closely approach realism. Sometimes simple lines of color suggest stylized features,[96] or a rolled piece of leather may be sewed on for a nose.[97] The more advanced forms display molded features, a nose with a flattened tip and wide nostrils, and lips fashioned with pleasing curves. The leather is molded while wet and allowed to dry in the desired form, then applied by tying with thongs through the mask itself.[98] Along the upper edge, horsehair is fastened to simulate the line of the hair. This 'wig,' when pulled back, may be clubbed into a knot at the back of the head or allowed to hang free. In this form of mask the Indian has definitely progressed toward realistic features and actual human contours. His painting, however, lacks reality. There is little attempt at natural tones, there is no blending of colors, and the designs possess the flat, geometric quality characteristic of woven textiles and the surface of pottery. On the other hand, and in a contrary direction, by the use of this same form the Indian has accomplished caricature and extreme exaggeration by the application of projecting snouts and bulging eyes, or horsehair beards, consistent, after all, with the fantasy of other Pueblo masks.

Helmet mask.—The simultaneous use of his two forms of masks, the strip and the bag, suggested to the inventive mind a third form, the helmet (pl. 13). By elongating the strip to encircle the head and then giving it a top like the bag, he had a mask which could rest on his head and shoulders and completely conceal his face and hair while at the same time it would provide space for more elaborate appendages on the outside. In the western pueblos the helmet masks have tops which round up over the head. Those found in the Rio Grande pueblos are flat.[99]

The helmet masks are made of heavy deerskin, buffalo hide, old Spanish saddle leather with the tooled markings of the Continental craftsmen turned inside,* or cowhide purchased nowadays from the local trader. After the skin is prepared, it is buried for hours in coarse wet sand in order to make it soft. The wearer's head is then measured and a rectangular strip is cut long enough to go around it and deep enough to cover the face. A circular piece is cut for the top. These are assembled and sewed with deer sinew, which is twisted by rolling it against the thigh. The sewing is very difficult and must be carefully done with small and close stitches in order to avoid tearing. The wet form is tried on the wearer and shaped in conformity with the contours of his head. When it is removed, the inside is smoothed and shaped by working it with a stick. It is then placed in the sun to dry beneath the kiva hatchway opening. Mouth and eye holes are next marked and cut. The deerskin thongs are adjusted: one on either side to tie under the chin, four pairs around the base with which to tie a separate collar in place, a pair at the top and one at the back for feather ornaments, and one or two pairs on each side for eartabs or appendages. A size of kaolin is rubbed over each mask to fill the pores and make it smooth, and over this the colors are applied either by blowing them on or by painting with rabbitskin swatches.[100]

---

* There are two such masks in the Fred Harvey Collection in Albuquerque, New Mexico.

There is one other mask form, which depends upon a slightly rounded plaque of basketry (pl. 14). This mask is put over the face and held in place by thongs around the head. It is finished at the back by a piece of cloth or deerskin which is fastened to the edge from side to side, crossing the top and completely covering the head.[101] Banded by a braid of corn-husk, in the periphery of which horsehair and feathers may be set, this mask displays ingenuity and cleverness. Undoubtedly other methods of construction are possible. One is to make an elongated base of small twigs or yucca leaves and cover it with leather or cloth (pl. 30); another is to shape leathers into other forms, such as the conical mask from Jemez. This is fashioned from one large triangular piece of leather in which the two long sides are sewn together, covered with a braid of cornhusk, and set with eagle feathers. It has a single slit for the eyes and is placed on the head with the point high in the air.[102]

Ornamentation of masks.—The secret of the changing personality of the performer is to be found in the ornamentation and the features applied to the masks. In the simpler forms the masks are constant, but they are always renovated before each dance and often are given a new character. The paint is scraped off and the appendages removed, new colors are applied, and snouts, eartabs, and ornaments are put on in conformity with what is prescribed by the dance to be performed and at the direction of the priest in charge of the ceremony.

The eyes of the mask are made by applying perforated leather circles (pl. 4), stuffed rims of leather or cloth, bulging wooden spheres, or cotton-stuffed knobs of deerskin (pl. 14). Mouths are made of jagged pieces of leather painted to suggest teeth, or braided cornhusk outlined with leather or fur. Snouts and beaks are made of corncobs or the round bodies or curved necks of gourds (pl. 13), or flat, round, or shaped pieces of wood or cottonwood root, all variously trimmed, cut, and painted to suggest

---

PLATE 27. *Deer dancer, San Juan. The more conventionalized forms result in further stylization.* ⟫⟶

Plate 27

teeth and lips. Snouts are often hollow, and this forms a resonance chamber for the actor, who as a kachina must voice no earthly sound. They may also be hinged to open and shut with a great clacking noise (pl. 7). Eartabs (pl. 4) are curved or square, large or small, of leather or wood. Their place is often taken by elaborate blossoms of colored yarn (pl. 9) or closed buds of painted wood edged with horsehair. Animal horns are pierced and fastened to the top of the mask, or imitation horns of the mountain sheep are ingeniously molded from deerskin (pl. 15); often substituted for horns are two matching gourd necks (pl. 35), or two slit ones, or two shaped strips of wood. The visors of the mask stand upright from the crown, or encircle the entire mask, or merely extend from side to side. They may be formed from crude strips of yucca bound together with braids of yucca cord,[103] or from neatly wound sections of coiled basketry[104] filled with kaolin and painted as a part of the mask (pl. 15).

Several masks have large terraced or scalloped tablets set upright over a helmet. A square opening is cut into the lower edge and this permits the tablet to fit down over the mask and be tied in place at the top and sides. These tablets are decorated with different painted designs and with ornaments of fluttering feathers and waving grasses (pl. 16).

Wooden ornaments are also used to enhance the decorative features of masks. Carved sticks are set vertically in the top, or zigzag strips, cut and painted to represent lightning, are fastened at the sides or upright at the back. The tops of the masks are covered with goatskin, horsehair, and various furs to simulate hair; evergreen to represent everlasting life; and raw cotton to suggest snow. The crown may be encircled with fillets of yucca leaves (pl. 24), twisted cornhusk, or spruce twigs.

Feather ornaments are numerous and are made in many different sizes, shapes, and combinations. Single tail feathers may be thrust through eartabs or tied upright at the back or sides, and downy white eagle feathers may wave from tablet points, visor rims, or topknots. One mask has eagle's down attached to the eartabs (pl. 15) so that the kachina may hear well;

"just as the downy feathers move in the slightest wind, so he can hear the smallest sound."[105] Long tail feathers are shaped into high, open fans standing upright at the back, or marching across the top from ear to ear, or forming a crest from front to back. Sheaves of feathers of various sizes, bound to a stick with wrappings of cotton cord, are sometimes fastened in a horizontal position at the top of the mask. One such sheaf is seen on the Salimapiya (pl. 5) as a special badge to denote the office of the wearer. Long, bright, parrot feathers, iridescent duck feathers, and gray-brown feathers of the sandhill crane are wound to a stick of sagebrush because "sagebrush is hard to get through and they want the Salimapiya to look dangerous."[106] Sometimes the head of a duck is mounted on the end of the stick. A similar ornament, utilizing the wing feathers of the eagle combined with white downy eagle and iridescent duck feathers fastened to a thin reed, is the "great feather" badge of the bow priest at Zuñi.[107] This is worn by warrior impersonators, and the direction in which the tips of the feathers point is believed to be prophetic. If they point backward the god will come in peace, but if they point forward he will come in a hostile mood. Other sheaflike ornaments are made of different feather combinations and tied upright at the side of a mask or at the back.

Very long feathers which project in opposite directions may be bound together in the center by their quill ends, and the joining covered by a bunch or topknot of small feathers. Or long feathers may be made to point at right angles to each other in four directions and the ends, curving upward, tipped with eagle's down. There are many loose pompons of small feathers (pl. 17), eagle's down, or the limber ends of larger feathers. Whenever the last-named are used, the ribs are slit and trimmed in order to make them quiver and dance in the breeze, or when the wearer moves in his routine dance pattern. These pompons are useful as topknots or as side or back ornaments, from which may rise a single feather or a gracefully fashioned sheaf.

Occasionally a crown of tall feathers, eagle or turkey, stands upright from the fillet of cornhusk about the upper edge of the mask, or a horizontal stick (pl. 3) with a series of feathers projecting at an angle may be worn forward from the center of the head, giving to the wearer a pompous and regal mien.

Occult symmetry is skillfully handled by the artistic Indian craftsman. For example, he places a long, pointed blue horn with a single fringe of black horsehair on one side of a mask, and balances it with a round, flat eartab of white broken by a horizontal black line, the whole completely surrounded by heavy fringes of horsehair in gleaming black. By carrying the black horizontal line of the ear across the mask to the eye, he is able to offset the simple square of the other eye, the blank space of vertical white, and the horizontal length and accent of color in the horn (pl. 3). The Indian uses the pointed bud of the Jimson weed (*Datura stramonium*) in the same manner. It sticks out on one side of a mask surrounded by red, dyed horsehair and is balanced by the heavily accented vertical line of two tall eagle feathers tied to the other side (pl. 13). Rarely, this symmetry is achieved by the use of color alone.

Unsymmetrical patterns, however, are not the usual forms. Bisymmetrical design is more common and can be seen in painted features or applied appendages. Variety is often obtained by the interchange of colors in exact space relations, as in the Humis mask, on one side of which the large, turquoise blue square is outlined in black and earth red while on the other the earth-red square is outlined in black and turquoise (pl. 16).

Small decorative designs painted on the masks may have a definite symbolic relation to the characterization. An example is the black chevron of the birds of prey (pl. 24) or the spots of color on the Zuñi Fire God. However, these designs are ordinarily nothing more than decorative pictures of rain, clouds, lightning, corn, frogs and tadpoles, bird tracks, feathers, or any number of other things executed in stylized form on pottery and altar slats as well as on masks. All these painted forms have their origin in the dependence of the Indian on the natural elements, sunshine and rain, for the germination and maturity of the corn and other vegetation. In some way each design is concerned with the constantly revolving pattern of life and the symbolism connected with it; the general and not the specific need is stressed.

On the masks of individual gods certain designs appear as marks of decoration and association rather than as symbols of characterization and identification. Often butterflies, frogs, dragonflies, and flowers are painted on the blank spaces just to make them pretty.

Noticeably ingenious and original is the manner in which the lower edge of the helmet mask is handled. Seldom is the appearance crude or unfinished. The desired elaboration is often accomplished by the use of those animal pelts which are plentiful, especially gray fox (pl. 29), coyote, mountain lion, rabbit, and goat; or great collars of evergreen (pl. 17) or feathers (pls. 5, 24) are used, which are effective but more difficult to construct. Occasionally a scarf of dark, native cloth, or an embroidered dance kilt is draped over the shoulders and fastened in front. A collar characteristic of Zuñi is a large roll of leather stuffed and painted either in a solid color or in black and white stripes (pl. 3). This same identifying feature is displayed on many Hopi masks the origin of which can be traced directly to Zuñi.

Sometimes the horsehair beard is used on the helmet mask; it then hangs down over the collar (pl. 35). On this kind of beard as used by the Hopi and the Zuñi are found horizontal strips of kaolin or eagle's down, stuck in place with yucca gum. Jemez displays beards of the hair of buffalo and bear, the latter with the center stained red.[108]

It is among the Hopi and the Zuñi that the craftsmanship and artistry of the Pueblo masks reach their highest development. Masks made in the villages of the Rio Grande are, by contrast, primitive, and lack variety.

The Indians hold in great reverence a certain type of sacred mask which, they believe, have been given them by the supernaturals. This

PLATE 28. *Deer dancer, Hopi. Complete stylization.*   》》》→

Plate 28

mask is owned by a clan and is handed down from one generation to another. To the household which keeps it, it is supposed to bring a sacerdotal distinction because of its power, and an eminence because of their knowledge of the secret rituals which concern it. Such masks are stored in sealed jars and are very carefully handled. They are considered 'dangerous' and must not be touched by those who are not in possession of their secrets. Although the masks may be renovated and redecorated, the individual characters which they depict are believed never to change.

Another type of mask is made for an individual and is owned exclusively by him. At Zuñi it is thought of as "his personal fetish so long as he lives, and is his guarantee of status after death."[109] Whenever a dance is performed, these masks are redecorated and made over into the likenesses of other supernaturals. In order that he may be able to take part in whatever dance is being performed, a man of standing owns several of these masks, one of each form. The masks are made by the priest, usually the kiva head, and his assistant, and they are made inside the kiva, where all their work is done. After the first ceremonial appearance of the mask, it may be taken home by its owner, and thenceforward it becomes his most prized possession. It is always treated with reverence and is kept in secret in the back room of his home. It is put on and taken off with the left hand only. If it needs to be renovated, he carries it to the kiva and does the work there.

There are two other masks, and they go a step beyond the scope of normal impersonation, becoming doubly effective because of their great stature and impressive bearing.[110]

At Zuñi there are six Shalako who are believed to be the messengers of the gods (pl. 7). They appear for the one great ceremony, the culminating event in the annual cycle of rites observed by the kachina priests. This occurs shortly after the winter solstice. Each of these giant figures is ten feet high. His huge blue mask, scaled to his size, has a long, hinged snout which clacks and clatters when operated by strings controlled by the wearer. The great, bulging, black and white eyes stare unblinkingly at the world. On each side of the mask is a long blue horn tipped with a downy red feather. A large fan-shaped crest of eagle feathers spans the head, and standing upright behind it is a sheaf of brilliant orange macaw feathers combined with downy white eagle feathers. The wig is of shiny black horsehair banged at the forehead, bobbed at the sides, and hanging down at the back with three puffs of eagle's down at intervals. The body, made on a series of hoops, is covered with two of the white ceremonial robes, a skirt and a mantle. A white embroidered kilt covers the top section, and two foxskins encircle the 'throat' below the ruff of glossy ravens' feathers. The tails of the foxskins serve as 'arms.' "The effigy worn by the Shalako is so ingeniously arranged that the wearer has only to step under the hoopskirt structure and carry it by a slender pole, which is supported by a piece of leather attached to the belt. The top of the blanket skirt has a triangular opening through which the bearer of the effigy sees."[111]

This same Shalako figure has been introduced from Zuñi to the Hopi. It is possible that the more ingenious western artists went further and produced a goddess who accompanied the Shalako god. In the Laboratory of Anthropology at Santa Fe there is a fine example of an antique head with the elaborate headdress of such a female effigy (pl. 18).[112] This head was no doubt carried above an impersonator and dressed in a feather robe with a white ceremonial mantle about its 'shoulders,' and adorned with many strings of beads about its 'neck.'[113] "The tablet represents terraced rain clouds . . . the object with bifid tips on each side of the tablet represents the squash blossom, symbolic of maidens' hair dress. Across the forehead is a symbol of an ear of corn, with two feathers attached to each end. . . . There are imitation flowers made of wood represented in the hair."[114] Each part of the tablet is separate, and it is either pegged to the main form or tied together with thongs.

PLATE 29. *Ahül, the Sun Kachina, Walpi, Hopi. Radiating eagle feathers represent the rays of the sun.*   ⟫→

Plate 29

PART FOUR

Costumes in Relation to the Prayer Drama

THE SOURCES for a study of the various costumes are fourfold. Individual garments may be seen and minutely examined in many museums and private collections. Long and exhaustive accounts of dances and rituals have been published in scientific reports dealing with anthropology, ethnology, and folklore. The costume descriptions are often detailed, and much can be learned by a comparison of the reports with photographs and illustrations. Indian artists have provided sketches and paintings which are very informative, particularly when carefully checked with authoritative reports. Carved wooden images, the so-called "kachina dolls" (pl. 2), afford valuable information in regard to the concept of masked mythological personages.[1] Most of these images come from Hopi and Zuñi, where they can be seen hanging from the roof beams in the pueblo homes. Several collections have been made and are accessible in museums. The dolls are carved from the root of the cottonwood tree and the art is of a primitive kind. "The representation of the body is subordinate to that of the head, often appearing as a shapeless imitation, but more generally as a conventionalized figure. . . . The characteristic details are always found on the head. The mask or helmet with its symbolic decorations was made to express characteristics of the Katcinas and care was given to delineate upon this part of the doll those features, or symbolic markings, by which they were distinguished."[2] Symbols painted on the head of a doll also appear on the mask of an impersonator of the same god.[3]

[177]

The Hopi dolls are squat and stolid, with characteristic garments carved into the wood. At Zuñi the figures are more slender in proportion, have articulate arms, and are dressed in actual pieces of cloth, fur, and leather. They also wear the characteristic feathers and head ornaments. They are painted with unsized earth pigments in the colors used by the dancing gods. These dolls are made by the men during retreat and later are given to the little girls on important ceremonial days. The child is permitted to carry the doll around for a few days; then it is hung to a rafter in the house, where it serves as a model by which the children come to identify the supernatural being it represents. There is evidence of the existence of a few of these dolls along the Rio Grande also,' but they are kept secret, as are the masked dances in which the gods appear.

ORIGIN OF CEREMONIAL COSTUME

One may well suppose that in prehistoric days the Indian made a special garment, the duplicate of his regular dress, which he put aside with great care to be worn only on those special occasions when he worshiped his gods. To make the garment more beautiful he probably whitened the firm cloth with powdered white clay and painted it with colors which seemed to him beautiful and which, in his mind, were associated with beautiful things. When he dressed in this costume, he would perhaps ornament it with a gay feather dropped by a passing bird or a flower newly bloomed by his doorstep. Evergreen branches made fitting tribute to gods eternal, and added color and beauty to the general scheme, so he may have placed them in his belt, or made wreaths for his shoulders, or carried them as bouquets in his hands. These customs doubtless endured for centuries. Then the Spaniards came, strong, hard men who ruled and killed. They were clothed from head to foot, making their bodies safe from many hardships. Through the years which followed, the Indian men began to copy the dress of the invaders. They had not the fine fabrics of the foreigners,

Plate 30. *Aholi, the Sun Kachina, Oraibi, Hopi. Elongated mask.*   ⟫⟩→

Plate 30

but they fashioned imitative garments from the clothes which they made. However, this did not change the costume set aside for the dance worship. In this the Indian continued as before, dressing as his gods had known him whenever he had sought their aid.

Then came drought and with it a state of great distress. Food was scarce, feathers became difficult to obtain, and animals went farther afield and could not be hunted down. We may assume that laxness in worship was held to be the reason for all these calamities, and the Indian then tried very hard to costume himself exactly as had his forefathers, so that the gods would be pleased and life would again be filled with plenty. The old priests surely remembered what colors were used and where the needled spruce was to be found. These things, they must have reasoned, the gods would like to see restored. They probably tried each magical arrangement, and when one brought success that arrangement became the rule. Even today, when the prayer drama is not successful and the reviving and cooling rain does not fall, they believe it is because something is amiss in the ceremony and the Great Ones are displeased. A chant may have been omitted, the colors may have run on a mask, or a man may not have been faithful to his vow of continence during the retreat.

FUNDAMENTAL CEREMONIAL COSTUME

The simplest ceremonial costumes are made up of the few garments that were worn before the white man came. An attempt to gain special favor with some god resulted in ornamentation that could be applied whenever dancing should be done for a particular result. Thus each drama calls for essential parts, distinguishing features worn or carried which differentiate one costume from another, making this one correct for the Bow Dance[5] and that for the Basket Dance.[6]

A step beyond this simple dress come those costumes which have added a fixed representative feature. The Tablita Dance, performed in many villages, makes use of a form of headdress from which it derives its name.

The tablita* is a flat wooden superstructure with the lower edge curved to fit across the head. It sits upright, the top cut in irregular forms, and soft feathers and the heads of beautiful wild grasses float from the points. Carried with majestic dignity, it is worn by the women dancers throughout a long, hot day of ceremony.

Among the Tewa the tablita appears in its simplest form (pl. 19). A turquoise blue plaque, painted sky-color, surmounts a head of glossy, floating hair. The top, terraced to suggest mesa and cloud, is accented by white feather puffs which represent prayers for the rain-bringing elements of nature. This touch of color enlivens the otherwise somber appearance of the women, who wear hand-woven dark dresses accented by a red belt bound around the waist. Heavy strands of turquoise and shell beads encircle the neck, and many bracelets of silver and turquoise band the arms. The bare feet scarcely leave the earth as the women move demurely, with downcast eyes, behind the men. A tight bunch of evergreen, clutched in each hand, adds the dull green of its stiff needles to this solemn scene— a scene which is nevertheless alive with color and movement, for the men (pl. 20), brilliant in their white kilts with jewellike colors, prance high, with black hair, fringe of rain sash, and pendent foxskin bounding with every step. Their hands and their bodies beneath the kilts are white. Bands of dark blue yarn are knotted at each knee, and turtle-shell rattles hang behind. White moccasins with skunk-fur heelpieces clothe the feet, and turquoise blue arm bands flaunt sprays of evergreens. The blackness of the loosened hair is accentuated by a yellow topknot of parrot feathers. Gourd rattles and sprigs of spruce are carried in the hands, moving up and down with each well-timed step.

In this dance, as observed in September, 1936, in San Ildefonso, the men and women come down the kiva steps and form casually into couples. two men followed by two women. The first figure of the dance is a forward step in a long, curved line about the plaza. In the center of the plaza

---

* *Tablita* is Spanish for "little tablet."

the chorus and the drummer stamp in time as they sing the mystic chant. On the side nearest the dancers a standard bearer takes up his position, holding a twenty-foot pole on the top of which is a banner surmounted by brilliant feathers. This he weaves slowly and continuously over the dancers.[7]

There are different tablita forms at Zuñi and Hopi, but the main costume is always the same.

A similar headdress usage is seen in connection with the Turtle Dance at San Juan,[8] where in a long file of men each wears an ornament of gourd fashioned into a blossom, with two eagle feathers, a macaw feather, and a sprig of evergreen sticking from it—the whole fastened to the top of the head in a horizontal position. There is only one exception to the usual costume: the fringe of the plaited sash, hanging down behind, takes the place of the customary pendent foxskin.

COSTUMES FOR IMPERSONATIONS

So far as interesting costume is concerned, the drama impersonations loom large beside these simple prayers in conventionalized dress.

The Pueblo Indian acquires ideas from almost everything with which he comes in contact. With him the mimetic art is a natural one: he can take on a new characterization as easily as he can put on a costume.

The rigid rules governing the significant use of certain garments and decorations have been mentioned before. Likewise, each impersonation has its own delineation and a prescribed pattern of action. When a serious variation occurs, a new person results. This correlation of costume and character is of some importance. There are so few actual garments that the arrangement of them is limited, yet the many hundreds of impersonations require careful delineation to distinguish one from another. The difference may be only the color of a mask or the shape of a feather ornament, each combined with significant ornamentation.

The earliest and most universal form of impersonation was effected by the use of cured animal heads and skins. "Impersonation of super-naturals is a religious technique world-wide in distribution. The two most common methods of impersonation are by animal heads and pelts, and by masks, but impersonation by means of body paint, elaborate costume and headdress, or the wearing of sacred symbols is by no means uncommon. In the pueblos, where all magic power is imputed to impersonation, all techniques are employed."[9]

Animal impersonations probably preceded all other impersonations. Animals were believed to be man's brothers, who by their existence made it possible for man to live. Animal headdresses and costumes were used as magic and decoy. By impersonating the animal he wished to kill, a hunter could come very close to a herd without being observed. By performing a dance before the hunt, the Hunt group believed that they could please the spirits of the animals, which would then permit their earthly bodies to be killed.

Many legends surrounding the animals form the background for these dramas. The dramas differ from one village to the next in conception of costume and in number and variety of characters. In the Buffalo Dance of San Juan there appear two Buffalo men and one Maiden,[10] whereas the San Ildefonso version requires two Buffalo men and two Maidens. Parsons says that on one occasion at Taos one hundred and forty Buffalo appeared with but two Deer characters.[11] Elk and Goat dances are also remarked, and some elaborate dramas include a large number of different beasts.

Buffalo Dance, San Ildefonso.—The Animal Dances are usually given in winter. That is the time of year for hunting because cultivated food is scarce and the animals are then forced down from their mountain homes. At San Ildefonso I saw a Buffalo Dance performed, contrary to custom, in August, 1936. The dancers, two men and two women, came from the round, outside kiva of the Turquoise people,[12] appearing through

PLATE 31. *Natacka Mother, Hopi. Female deity impersonation.*   ⟫⟫→

Plate 31

the hatchway about mid-morning. The bodies (pl. 21) of the men were painted a dark earth brown with white crosses on each side of the chest and abdomen and on each arm. They wore soft, cream-colored deerskin kilts, with a writhing black serpent painted through the center, and a border of blue and yellow the bottom of which was edged with metal tinklers, small cones of tin which hung from deerskin thongs and knocked together with every rhythmic movement of the dancers, making a pleasing, silvery sound. A red woven belt held the kilt in place, and a string of bells around the waist added a deeper, more musical tone, punctuating the less melodic vibrations of rattles and drums. Below the knee the legs were encircled by bands of brown buffalo hair which sustained, in front, a floating eagle feather. White moccasins with buffalo-hair heelpieces encased the feet. Arm bands were of buffalo hair. Several strands of white shell beads were worn around the wrists, and many necklaces of turquoise and white shell were around the neck. Just under the chin was a large abalone shell. A gourd rattle with a fringe of bright orange-dyed goat's hair was carried in the right hand, and evergreen and a bow and arrow with four eagle feathers swinging from the string appeared in the other. A large piece of the heavy neck fur of the buffalo over the head and shoulders made a shaggy frame for the little that could be seen of the face. The horns on each side had eagle's down fluttering from their tips. On the back of the buffalo headdress, moving gracefully up and down, was an ornament composed of a fan of eagle wing and macaw tail feathers with the quill ends covered with orange-dyed goat's hair and a large bunch of green and yellow parrot feathers. A small downy white feather was tied directly on top.

The Buffalo Maidens (pl. 22), impersonating the mothers of the game animals, appeared in dresses made from large, hand-woven, white cotton blankets embroidered at top and bottom. Over this, like a short tunic, was a man's embroidered white dance kilt. Both dress and tunic were fastened on the right shoulder. The panel of stylized cloud, rain, and earth symbols made a line of decoration from shoulder to waist. The great wrapped moccasins of soft white deerskin gave a modest air to the costume, and the heelpieces of black and white skunk fur rounded it off. White shell beads were wound around the wrists, and strings of turquoise and white shells hung in heavy festoons on the breast. A necklace of turquoise with an entire abalone shell encircled the base of the neck. Arm bands of brilliant orange-dyed goat's hair made blobs of color midway in the figure. The black hair hung loose in a solid gleaming mass, while in direct contrast a downy white eagle feather floated from the top. At the back an ornament rose from the neckline majestically above the head. It was composed of a great bunch of green and red parrot feathers, edged in orange-dyed goat skin, supporting three macaw tail feathers—scarlet shafts of color. In each hand formal bouquets were carried. These were composed of shining eagle and parrot feathers surrounded by the dull green of spruce needles and edged with creamy white olive shells[13] which added beauty and supplied a clicking accompaniment to the rhythmic accent of the rattles.

Each dancer was in character from the moment he appeared above the rim of the kiva. With lowered eyes, the men danced with a heavy, steady, downward beat. They were young men, their bodies full of vigorous strength. Their movements, however, were not excessive, but poised and controlled in easy, graceful posture. The maidens were young and handsome. Their clear brown skins were ruddy with health and this contrasted strongly with the positive whiteness of their garments and the jet blackness of their hair. They danced demurely with downcast eyes. Their steps echoed rather than followed those of the men. Never by glance or movement did they betray a consciousness of the spectators, who might crowd in closely. Between the dance patterns the performers were in constant movement, their tinklers rattling and their bodies intent on the regular motion of a stately trot. Their leader, a priest in the somber pueblo dress of the conquistadors, was almost concealed by his great blanket. He carried a feather insigne and sprinkled meal for the dancers' 'road'. The chorus was made up of a knot of men, grouped on one side, who danced gently to the rhythm of their own chants. In their midst a large drum was beaten with hypnotic cadence.

The Buffalo Dance, Tesuque.—In the Tesuque Buffalo Dance a group of men and women, numbering eighteen couples in all, perform an entire routine as a frame for three dancers and their leaders. These line dancers—if one may call them so for convenience—come from one kiva and perform in the dance places around the village. Returning to the plaza, they stand in two lines facing each other. Here they are joined by the five Buffalo Dancers: two men in buffalo costumes and a woman in a white embroidered

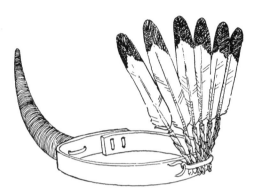

FIGURE 25. Headdress of the side dancers, Buffalo Dance. Six eagle feathers bound with cornhusks and a buffalo horn are tied to a deerskin with thongs.

mantle dress constituting the group of three, and two other men, one the father or leader and the other the hunter. This second group performs a serpentine between the two stationary lines.

The costumes of the line dancers are significant in reflecting the qualities of both the Buffalo impersonations and the usual ceremonial attire, a uniform which contributes to the particular performance and yet keeps its place as a subordinate element. When I saw them, the men dancers wore rough buckskin kilts, with belts and anklets of bells, and low moccasins with skunk heelbands. A blackened horn projected from the right side of the head, while on the left was a fan of six or more eagle tail feathers. Both these decorations were attached to a beaded headband.[14] The hair was queued or short. Thin strips of pelt hung from the arm and leg bands. In the right hand was a gourd, in the left a bow and arrow. The upper and lower parts of the face were painted black, with a broad red stripe across the bridge of the nose. In one dance line the bodies were blackened, in the other they were painted red. On the backs were splotches of white paint, and the thighs, forearms, and hands were whitened.[15]

Dance of the Game Animals, San Felipe.—The drama of the many horned animals includes all those who, friendly to the Indian, formerly provided him with food during the long winters. The actors are clothed to impersonate the buffalo, deer, mountain sheep or elk, and antelope,[16] as these were the principal game animals of the region surrounding the ancient Pueblo lands.

The San Felipe play begins at dawn when a lovely dark-skinned maiden runs swiftly toward the mountains behind the pueblo. She is the chosen mother of the animals, and she goes to lure them into the village. She is accompanied by young men dressed as hunters, in white buckskin garments similar to those of the Plains Indians. They carry bows and arrows and sprigs of evergreen. All the young people chosen for this part of the ceremony must be fleet and sure of foot, for their purpose is to run as fast as the beasts and drive them into the village amid the great applause of the spectators.

There follows a secret rite in one of the ceremonial chambers, and the entire group emerges to continue the action of the play and to dance in the plaza, where small evergreen trees have been set up to suggest a forest. Each group, including a scattering of hunters, interprets the movements of the beasts they are impersonating. The Buffaloes, with black bodies, deerskin kilts, and heavy, shaggy buffalo headdress, dance with the solid weight of large and lumbering animals.[17] The Buffalo Maiden dances just behind the leader, her white dress banded at the waist by a red woven belt. On her head is a tight cap covered with iridescent black feathers and topped by the two small horns of the buffalo cow. Her legs are wrapped in high white moccasins ending in skunk-fur heelpieces. Quantities of

PLATE 32. *Natacka Daughter, Hopi. Female deity.*   ⟫⟫→

Plate 32

turquoise and white shell beads hang around her neck. In one hand she carries a rattle wand to which are attached feathers, evergreen sprigs, and animal hoofs.

Next come the Elk, lofty and regal in their horned headdresses; and then the antlered Deer approach quickly with shy and fugitive grace. Bird down and puffs of cotton trim the prongs of horns and antlers, and from their foreheads fan-shaped visors of slender sticks rise upward and forward. A red fringe of goat's hair covers the quill ends of an eagle-feather ornament which is tied, tip downward, on the hair at the nape of the neck, and sprigs of evergreen fall over the shoulders. White shirts cover the bodies, and from waist to knee are kilts either of dark blue native stuff with a red and green strip through the middle, or of Hopi-embroidered white cotton cloth. Around the waist the white plaited sashes with tasseled ends are knotted at the back to suggest the tails of the animals. White, crocheted leggings, tied at the knee with red yarns, end in low moccasins edged with black and white skunk-fur heelpieces. A light, short stick is carried, and it is decorated with a spray of evergreen which is bound to the center with cotton cord. These sticks are used to support the weight in different postures and to imitate the movement of the forefeet of the animal when running or leaping.

The Mountain Sheep appear with giant horns rising on either side of the caplike base. The Antelope wear on their bodies snug-fitting suits with the backs painted yellow and bellies white to simulate the animal's skin. On the heads are antelope horns. They frisk gaily, their feather tails bobbing up and down. The impersonators dance upright, often leaning forward to rest on the canelike props.

Interrupting the last dance, the animals break away and run for the hills. When they are 'shot down' (that is, when they are caught by townsmen or hunters) they lie inert and 'dead' while they are carried to the kiva across the hunters' backs. The successful hunter receives a spray of evergreen for his reward.

The Eagle Dance.—In his dramatizations the Pueblo Indian represented birds as well as animals. He watched the eagle soaring overhead. This was the one bird which, with his great, strong wings, could fly out of sight in the blue upper distances. Certainly he must fly to the very sun, and surely he had direct intercourse with the Sky Powers and told the Great Father all that befell his human children! Hence, the Eagle impersonation has become very important and is often connected with medicine and curing.[18]

This dance drama expresses the supposed relationship between eagle and man and the deific powers.* It is performed by two young men, who, costumed to represent eagles, faithfully imitate the birds' movements.

The keynote of the eagle dress is stylized realism (pl. 23). The gleaming brown-black of the upper body is interrupted by a vest-shaped patch of bright yellow on the chest. This is outlined with eagle down. The lower arms, legs, and bare feet are as yellow as the legs and talons of an eagle, and the face is yellow with a brilliant red patch across the chin. The smart, soft, buckskin kilt, the color of cream, displays through the center an undulating snake design, and at the bottom of the kilt are strips of blue, yellow, and black, while the tinklers, made of tin and forming the fringe, click together throughout the dance. This garment is held in place by a leather belt of turquoise blue banded by a string of sharp-toned brass bells; the body beneath is painted white. Sprays of spruce stick up above the waist. A sweeping, fan-shaped tail of eagle feathers is attached at the back, and perfectly fashioned wings of long eagle feathers, bound to a strip of heavy buckskin, cover the arms and shoulders from finger tip to finger tip. The hair hangs loose, and the head is covered with white down or raw cotton, forming a deep, snug cap, to which a long, yellow beak is fastened so that it protrudes just above the wearer's nose.

It is obvious that the dancers have made a close study of the eagle's flight, so exact are they in the reproduction of the movements. They

---

* In the eastern pueblos it is always preceded by fasting and retreat.

create the illusion of soaring through the clouds, hovering over the fields, and perching on high aeries. Again, they strut along the ground, or fiercely swoop, or circle wildly—their bells tinkling like rain—as if disturbed by an approaching storm.

When women accompany the Eagle men in the dance, they are beautifully garbed in snowy white dresses, fringed sashes, and moccasins, accented with jet black embroidered bands, skunk fur, and gleaming hair.[19] Black and white eagle feathers are carried in each hand, and form an ornament at the back of the neck where the only relief in color harmony is the long, tapering points of yellow macaw feathers set at equal distances around a plaque and showing like a halo behind the head.

A further step in the process of impersonation is the masked being. We do not know whether this grew out of the animal and bird characterizations, but it is interesting to contrast the masked and unmasked representation of the same character in two villages so similar in material ways of life. The Rio Grande Eagle appears real and natural beside the Hopi Eagle (pl. 24), yet their origin is the same. They were nurtured on the same beliefs, and they developed with similar objectives. The Rio Grande Eagle wore a kilt of buckskin because the beautiful, soft-tanned hides from the plains were accessible to him. The Hopi Eagle, on the contrary, wore a kilt of native cotton which the Hopi cultivated and wove into cloth. The distinguishing body paint, kilt, brocaded sash, woven red belt, and pendent foxskin are the conventional items of dress for the masked supernatural, and the anklets, wound in colored yarns, are typical of Hopiland. The Hopi eagle wings are more carefully designed and have greater perfection of finish. The rough leather, where the quills of the long wing feathers are fastened, is covered with white down. On the back is a long, flat plaque or shield of buckskin edged in red horsehair, for "the eagle is the chief of birds, and so he wears the shield on his back."[20] At length there is the mask, a distorted object which does not resemble man, and which resembles a bird in nothing but the yellow hooked beak in front. The helmet of leather, painted the sacred turquoise blue, has large projecting red tab ears and round black and white wooden eyes. The black chevron above the snout is always found on the masks of certain birds of prey.[21] Around the crown is a green yucca fillet tied in front, and from the top wave long, downy white eagle feathers and red and yellow parrot feathers. At the back, two tall black and white eagle feathers stand upright from a great pompon of small black and white feathers which is a part of the full and beautiful collar of like material.

Introduced from Hopi to Zuñi, the Eagle Dance in both villages is a prayer that the eaglets in the nests on the rocky mesa ledges may be increased in number, so that there will be a plentiful supply of fine feathers for the garments of the supernaturals in the other world.[22]

COMPARISON OF STYLE

Animal impersonations show also a development from the primitive forms to the more highly symbolic and artistic ones—from the realistic to the stylized.

Taos.—The Animal Dance as given at Taos (pl. 25) represents one of man's earliest efforts at mimetic magic. Here the impersonator of the Deer wears the head and entire skin of the carefully cured and preserved animal. "The head of the animal is over the dancer's head, the pelt hanging down his back."[23] The spectator is hardly conscious of the men's faces as they bend over two sticks which represent the animal's forelegs. A dark kilt and low moccasins complete the costume. There is little color; the sandy gray-brown hair on the back blends into the white of the bellies. Above the head rise the colorless, sharply pointed horns, and from the mouths of the animals sticks jauntily the deer's favorite food, the tender tips of the dark green spruce.[24]

PLATE 33. *Natacka Man, Hopi. This is the bogeyman of all Hopi children. A deerskin mantle is worn over the right shoulder. The great snout is made of gourd halves hinged together.*   ⟫→

Plate 33

San Ildefonso.—San Ildefonso (pl. 26) offers the next attempt at styliza-tion.[25] Here the impersonator has emerged from the hide and retains only the antlers supported on a tight-fitting cap, from which hangs a sheaf of feathers. The dancers of this pueblo have also retained the ears and two canes for the front feet. An irregular visor of thin sticks has developed in front, topped by eagle's down, and sprays of evergreen hang over each shoulder. The face is painted black with an edge of white; the hands are whitened. A white shirt covers the upper body, which was probably nude until a few years ago. The kilt may be of dark blue native cloth or white Hopi cotton, and the plaited sash hangs down the back. Crocheted leg-gings, held in place by strands of red yarn at the knee, end in white moc-casins and skunk-fur heelpieces.

San Juan.—The Deer of San Juan (pl. 27) suggests a further step in styl-ization and a tendency to vary the detail. The close gray cap, tied under the chin, is dotted with eagle's down, and the antlers rise high on either side. A wide, high visor of thin yucca strips fans out around the head and destroys much of the quiet, deerlike quality. The rear of the buckskin cap tapers low over the queued knot of shiny hair and supports a wide semicircle of long eagle feathers held in place by a cornhusk ring, like a half sun-disk hanging down over the shoulder. The body is covered with a white shirt and a white kilt. The embroidered panel of the kilt is worn at the back and is somewhat concealed by the long, loose fringe of the plaited white sash knotted above it. White crocheted leggings, with bells at the knees and fringes of white cord down the front, and white moc-casins with skunk-fur heelpieces complete this dress of predominant black and white. A tall staff, with three eagle feathers and an evergreen bound to the top with cotton cord, is carried in one hand, and a gourd rattle in the other. The action of the dancers is much stiffer and more convention-alized, and the animallike movements are only suggested. The dance pattern is a mere formality, and the sticks become a decoration, losing entirely their significance as the forelegs of an animal.

Hopi.—Further degrees of stylization are seen in the Deer impersonations of Jemez,[26] Zuñi,[27] and Hopi,[28] among those masked figures which appear with all the animals in the mixed dances.[29] The simplest mask is seen at Jemez: a round green helmet of deerskin, with a flat top, from which deer horns are projected, as well as two pointed ears fashioned from leather. An evergreen collar is around the neck.[30]

At Hopi the Deer dancer (pl. 28), like the Eagle dancer, has the usual brilliant body paint, the white embroidered ceremonial kilt, white sash with brocaded ends, red woven belt, and pendent foxskin. His moccasins are of red-brown deerskin, with ankle fringes of the same material. The mask is a turquoise blue helmet with a black center and rectangular, wide, black eyes. Around the top is a low visor made from slit yucca leaves and painted yellow and red. A long, flat, black snout projects in front. On each side are squash-blossom ornaments, made of yarn wound over little sticks and forming wide, flat cones. At the back, standing upright from a bunch of owl's feathers, are two tall eagle feathers. They represent a prayer for rain. The only elements remotely related to the deer are the two horns fastened to the top of the mask. Everything else has been exaggerated or bears relationship only to the stipulated pattern of ceremonial dress. This, although aesthetically satisfactory, destroys all illusion of realism. The Indian desired this of his masked figures; since they are supernatural, they should not appear like human beings.

In many villages the characters of the ceremonial dramas surrounding these gods are often similar. However, each pueblo prescribes its own rules for costume and action, so that they do not appear alike even when borrowed. The masked figure symbolizes, to the Indian, a kind and gentle people who are fond of singing and dancing and whose greatest concern is the welfare of the human race. That is why there is no feeling of terror for them; the kachinas inspire only respect and honor.

PLATE 34. *Tümas, the Mother of the Floggers, Hopi. The mask is trimmed with crow's wings.*   »»→

Plate 34

The number of masked impersonators is almost unlimited. New characters are added from year to year and ancient ones are often revived. Many characters are presented by groups to whom they were eventually handed down by clans now extinct.[31] This assured to the favored pueblo, throughout many generations, the benefits of the power and goodness attributed to the kachinas thus bequeathed. Whenever the costume and distinctive traits of a character become defined, that character is handed down, together with whatever ritual and legend surround him. The knowledge of this mass of ritual and legend in all its complexity gave preëminence to the office of priest, for only through him could the information be perpetuated. There are both individual and group characterizations. The individual is the only one of his kind and he has a special part to play; the group consists of a large number, all alike and appearing together in dance and song. The size of the groups depends upon the number of men who are able to participate and who desire to do so.

A description of certain important and typical ceremonies may make clear the action as well as the appearance of some of the supernatural characters. They are representative of kachina types and illustrate the various methods by which characterization is obtained.

CEREMONIAL POWAMU, HOPI

Among the Hopi the calendric cycle of ceremonies includes a series of extended festivals, each made up of kiva rites, prayers, and dances. The festivals differ upon the three mesas; certain interpretations of costume and ritual appear to have occurred independently in each village.

Throughout a period of sixteen to twenty days of the second moon after the winter solstice, Powamu, the bean-planting ceremony, celebrates the return of the kachinas, who have been away from Hopiland since July. This festival also involves the exorcism of evil spirits from youth and man, and is appropriately placed in our month of February[32] to denote the purification and renovation of the earth for future planting.[33]

The Powamu ceremony is one of the most important and interesting festivals held on the Hopi mesa, and because it is the occasion of the advent of the supernaturals, many masked figures 'visit' the pueblo. Ordinarily, the commencement of a ceremony is proclaimed from the housetops, but for Powamu a messenger is sent from kiva to kiva to announce quietly and formally that the festival is soon to begin—a procedure required by a convention that no kachina names are spoken in public.[34] During the next few days, prayer sticks are made for placing at various shrines, and the painting and renovation of masks begins. The masks are brought out of their storage jars, the old paint is scraped off, new colors are applied, designs are painted on, and the proper feather ornaments are assembled. In the evenings dance groups from the various kivas make the rounds and entertain audiences in each ceremonial chamber. Fewkes describes such a festival as follows: "On every evening from the opening to the close of the festival there were dances, unmasked and masked, in all the kivas of the East Mesa. . . . The unmasked dances of the katcinas in the kivas are called by the same names as when masks are worn. Some of them are in the nature of rehearsals. When the dances take place in the public plaza, all the paraphernalia are ordinarily worn, but the dances without masks in the kiva are supposed to be equally efficacious."[35]

Early in the festival, beans and corn are planted in basins of sand in all the kivas. The seeds are then forced to germinate by frequent watering and continuous heat. The fire beneath the hatchway is kept burning day and night, and a straw mat placed over the opening retains the heat, making the room a "veritable hot house."[36]

One morning, just as the eastern sky reddens with the dawn, Ahül, the Sun Kachina (pl. 29),[37] comes up the trail, with his great circular mask radiating eagle feathers like the rays of the sun. He is accompanied by the kachina chief. In the capacity of leader of the returning kachinas, the

PLATE 35. *Black Tungwüp, the Flogging Kachina, Hopi. The kilt is made of horsehair dyed red.*   ⟫⟫→

Plate 35

former visits each kiva, bestowing prayers and blessings and presenting gifts of corn and bean sprouts to the kiva groups in retreat.

At Walpi this character wears around his waist an embroidered dance kilt painted with a turquoise blue border and held in place by a brocaded sash over which is looped a red woven belt. A pendent foxskin is behind. His feet are covered with blue and red dance moccasins, and the leggings have a row of shell tinklers down the sides. Woven red garters band the knees, and blue yarn is tied around each wrist. In one hand he carries a squirrelskin bag of meal, a bundle of bean and corn sprouts, a chief's insigne, and a small slat of wood dentate at each end. In the other hand is a tall staff, the top decorated with eagle feathers and horsehair, while an ear of corn and a crook are attached midway. His discoidal face mask has a buckskin head covering at the back and a foxskin collar. The disk is divided horizontally in half. In the lower part, which is painted black, there is a protruding beak, above which is painted a black triangle. The upper half is divided vertically by a black line; the left side is yellow, the right side green. Both areas are covered with small black crosses. Around the upper side is a periphery of long eagle feathers and red horsehair, held in place by a braid of cornhusk.[38]

The corresponding character at Oraibi (pl. 30) is called the Aholi, and is thus described by H. P. Voth: "The Aholi paints his body as follows: Both upper arms, the sternum, abdomen, back and legs down to the knees, bright red. The left shoulder and breast, right arm and lower part of the right leg, and a narrow band or ring above the right knee and a similar band below the left knee, yellow. The right shoulder and breast, lower arm, lower part of left leg and a band above the left and one below the right knee, blue. . . . The Aholi is dressed in the regular katcina kilt and sash, a woman's sash [red woven belt] and moccasins. Over the shoulders he wears an old [antique] blanket made of native cotton cloth on which are drawn designs of clouds and other unidentified objects. In the center is a large drawing of the mythical being that has been observed on different ceremonial objects. The head is human, the body that of a large bird.[39] . . . In the right hand the Aholi holds a stick, to the upper end of which six makwanpis* are attached. . . . The mask of the Aholi is also rather plain. It is made of yucca leaves and covered with native cotton cloth. To the lower edge is tied a foxskin, while to the apex are fastened a number of feathers of various kinds and to the sides a blossom symbol."[40]

An occasion of the ceremony most dreaded, especially by the young, is the advent of the monsters, the Natackas. These are horrible creatures who threaten and frighten those who have misbehaved at any time during the year. They are the bogeymen of all little Hopi children. They make two visits, the first early in Powamu, when they come to demand food which will be collected on their second visit, which is on the last day. The night before each visit, they are announced by a loud dialogue in which they demand to see the children. The kiva chief replies that they must wait because everyone is at home asleep. The following day they parade through the streets, threatening the villagers, and frightening the children and accusing them of their misdeeds. The food, or spoils, is gathered up by one or two Hehea (pl. 4) who accompany the Natackas.

The Natacka Mother (pl. 31), impersonated by a man, wears a woman's dark dress. A white brocaded sash is wrapped twice around the body so that the many-hued ends meet and fall at angles down the front, making a brilliant herringbone of color. The sash is held in place by a red woven belt. A maiden's blanket, woven of native white cotton with red and blue borders, is thrown about the shoulders. The feet and legs are covered with soft white wrapped leggings, and the hands are whitened. A supple foxskin collar hides the lower edge of a helmet mask which has on its face an inane expression; the character is supposedly stupid. Black human hair, twisted into rolls, hangs down on each side like the Hopi matron's coiffure. A thin red horsehair fringe veils the face, and a topknot of square-tipped turkey feathers flutters from the apex.[41]

---

* An aspergillum used in connection with the Medicine Bowl.

The Natacka Daughter (pl. 32), smaller and more active, also appears in a dark dress, a red belt, and white wrapped moccasins. Over her shoulders like a cape she wears a streaked buckskin mantle. Her unpleasant face mask has round green eyes and a straight mouth edged in red, with jagged teeth. A black horsehair beard hangs beneath. The real hair of the boy who is impersonating the character hangs loose, and at the front is smeared with white clay. The Natacka Daughter is supposed to be disreputable and slovenly. On her back she carries a basket by means of a cord passed over her head. This is to contain the food as it is gathered by the Heheas.

The male Natackas (pl. 33) wear light shirts, dark trousers, and red-brown buckskin leggings held up by red woven garters. Their feet are covered by ordinary moccasins. Soft buckskin mantles pass under the left arm and are fastened on the right shoulder, and the hands are whitened except where the paint is removed by drawing the fingers across their backs, leaving a definite design. The awe-inspiring helmet masks have large open snouts with pointed teeth. The bulging black and white eyes appear to spring away from their dark background, and the sharp feather-tipped horns add to the frightening effect. A fan-shaped crest of eagle feathers, bristling with animosity, stands upright at the back, and a trifid design painted[42] on the forehead suggests deep and scowling ill-humor.

During the several days of retreat the men make kachina dolls for the girls and miniature bows and arrows for the boys. These are given to the children at the last performance. The masks used in the night dances are always redecorated by day. On the day set aside for this purpose the women renovate the kiva by replastering the walls with a thin wash of adobe mud, thus keeping it fresh and clean.

Every four years, children between the ages of six and ten years are initiated into the kachina group[43] at a rite which occurs during Powamu. This rite is observed in one of the kivas. Tümas, a kachina woman, and her two sons, the Black Tungwüp and the Blue Tungwüp, participate.

The masked figure of Tümas (pl. 34), impersonated by a man, wears a woman's dark dress, and a white plaited sash with a long fringe is knotted on the right side. A hand-woven white cotton mantle, embroidered with brilliantly colored borders, is thrown over the shoulders. Tümas carries a sheaf of long, dull green, yucca leaves. Her turquoise blue helmet mask has a double triangular face design in black, edged with white—an effective balance of dark, middle, and light values. On either side of this mask, tied in a vertical position, is an appendage of crisp black feathers—the entire wing of the impertinent crow. A topknot of gayly colored parrot feathers forms the apex of the mask."

The Tungwüp (pl. 35), her two sons, act as floggers. They are often dressed in costumes exactly alike. Their bodies are covered with dull black paint, upon which appear occasional small circles of white kaolin, emphasized by fluffs of eagle down stuck to the centers. The forearms, chests, and lower legs are painted yellow, and white is applied to the hands and the bodies beneath the lower garments. An unusual form of kilt, consisting of a deep fringe of horsehair stained red, is worn around the waist and held in place by a leather belt of turquoise blue. This color combination is striking and effective, and the long strands of wiry horsehair fall in graceful shapes around the bare, painted legs of the dancer, who is in constant rhythmic agitation. The ends of the ever-present breechclout form a decorative part of this body covering. These are drawn out over the top of the kilt and belt, and hang in front and back like small, dark blue aprons, with cords of green and red yarn tracing a square in the lower section. Arm bands of turquoise blue leather, worn above the elbow, have tassels of green yarn and floating eagle feathers hanging from their outer sides. Strands of dark blue wool are tied below the knees, the loops swinging in front. Tortoise-shell rattles, hanging over the calf of each leg, emphasize every movement with sound. Red-brown moccasins are worn, with anklets of fringed red-brown deerskin, adding

PLATE 36. *Blue Tungwüp, the Alternate Flogger, Hopi.*   ⟫⟫→

Plate 36

a rich accent at the feet. In both hands are carried whips of lithe, tapering yucca leaves which are used in the initiation ceremonies.

The mask which accompanies this costume is a leather helmet painted shiny black. A long, black, curved horn of gourd, with traceries of turquoise blue, sticks out from either side. Eagle feathers, tied with the soft twist of native cotton cord, trail from the center of each horn. The eyes, which are bulging black and white wooden spheres, stare out of the flat brilliance of the surface. Across the lower edge of the masks is a leather strip forming a wide, many-toothed mouth with a border of red, from the bottom of which hangs a black horsehair beard striped with three horizontal bars of white paint. At the apex of the mask, extending backward, is a fan-shaped ornament of eagle feathers, the quill ends hidden by a brilliant topknot of parrot feathers. A glossy gray foxskin collar covers the neck space between mask and body.

When the characters of the two floggers differ, the second is represented by the Blue Tungwüp (pl. 36). His body, like that of the Oraibi Aholi, is painted in three colors: yellow on the left shoulder, the right forearm, and the left lower leg; blue on the right shoulder, the left forearm, and the right lower leg; and red on the torso, the upper arms, and the upper legs. The hands are white. Around the waist is the usual embroidered white kilt, many-colored brocaded sash, and red woven belt with a pendent foxskin. Red-brown moccasins with fringed anklets are on the feet, and strands of blue yarn are around the legs. Above the elbow are turquoise blue arm bands, and the costume is completed with a wristlet of yarn and a bow guard. He carries smooth, slender yucca leaves. The mask, similar to that of the Black Tungwüp, is painted turquoise blue with the same designs traced along the black horns, and the same eagle feathers and brilliant topknot.

Mr. Voth's description of the rites[45] enables us to follow the ceremonial procedure on this day when the small neophytes are initiated into the secret cult of the Kachinas.

In the morning, colored sands are procured from the dry jars in the inner rooms of the chief's house, where treasures are carefully stored. A space about four feet square is cleared on the floor, and selected men, who know the ritual, begin the arduous process of creating a sand painting which is used only on this particular day and is destroyed before the sun dips below the blue outline of the San Francisco Peaks to the west. "They first sift a layer of common yellow sand on the floor, three-quarters to one inch thick. This is thinly covered with a layer of light brown ochre [and] on this field are then produced three figures," the flogging kachinas and their mother.[46] On each side appear the Tungwüp, black figures with white arms and legs, red fringe kilts, and black heads with horns and feathers. In each hand are long yucca leaves. The central figure represents Tümas, and she is dressed in a black dress, white sash and mantle, and a blue head with side appendages and a white topknot. Over the field are spots of different colors which represent herbs and blossoms.[47]

A second and smaller sand painting is made by the Powamu priest in the afternoon. It represents Shipapu, the place from which the human family is believed to have emerged. On an ocher background is described a square of different colors representing the four different quarters: yellow, north; blue-green, west; red, south; and white, east. Each side has, in directional color, a terraced figure which is said to "represent the blossoms of Shipapu." Lying on each side is an ear of corn and a celt or stone implement, both of which are colored to correspond to the direction, like the figures.

After the preparations have been made, a short kiva ritual is performed. The three impersonators then go to another room to put on their costumes. "By this time the children who are to be initiated begin to arrive. Each has a white corn ear and is accompanied by two persons, one male and one female, who may be either married or single. They are said to 'put in,' i.e. to introduce or initiate the young into the katcina order. . . . When they arrive with their candidate they all sprinkle a pinch of corn meal on the natsi* and, having descended the ladder, sprinkle meal also on the small sand mosaic; whereupon the candidate is requested to step into . . . a yucca-leaf ring or wheel.† . . . Two men, squatting on opposite sides, hold this ring and, when the candidate is standing in it, raise and lower it four times, expressing at the same time the wish that the [child] may grow up and live to an old age and always be happy. [The] candidate is then taken by his sponsor . . . into the north part of the kiva; another one follows and so on until all have gone through the same performance."[48] This is followed by the entrance of the Powamu priest, who comes down the ladder and takes his place on one side. As the God of Germination and Growth, he tells of his mythical wanderings and his final safe arrival in the pueblo. This long, rhythmic chant is full of the beauty and imagery of the Indian legends, colored by their aesthetic appreciation of nature. At its close he goes among the people, sprinkling the heads of the young candidates with 'medicine.' As he climbs the ladder to depart, four Mud-heads appear and conduct a short ceremony at the small sand painting, using the objects which lie on each side in a ritualistic manner.

A sudden noise is heard above the hatchway. The great moment has arrived! Accompanied by loud hooting and the clatter of rattles, the two floggers and their mother descend the ladder. With Tümas near them, the Tungwüps take their positions on either side of the large sand painting. Throughout their part in the ceremony they keep up a continuous howling, grunting, rattling, and brandishing of yucca leaves. The candidate is placed on the sand painting and, if a boy, divested of his clothes; only the shawls of the little girls are removed. The candidate is then given four or five lashes by one of the Tungwüps, who relieve each other at the task of flogging, often exchanging their cudgels for new ones from the supply borne by Tümas. Many of the older people present their arms and legs for the beneficial blows. The flogging is performed for the purpose of purification, but it also suggests a punishment which may be meted

---

* Society emblem at the hatchway. † Four lengths of yucca leaves tied together.

out to any initiate who betrays his knowledge of the secret rites and beliefs which are soon to become so important a part of his life. Now the
initiate is to learn the supernatural myths, to dance when rain is needed,
and to become powerful through the knowledge of prayer and rite by
which the gods of his universe are approached.

The many kachinas who return to wander about the villages and dance
on the days when no specific public rituals are scheduled, are not always
the same from year to year. "Of the masked personations among the Hopi,
some, as Tungwüp, Ahül, and Natacka, always appear in certain great
ceremonies at stated times of the year. Others are sporadic, having no
direct relation to any particular ceremony, and may be represented in
any of the winter or summer months. They give variety to the annual
dances, but are not regarded as essential to them, and merely to afford
such variety many are revived after long disuse. Each year many katcinas
may be added to any ceremony from the great amount of reserve material
with which the Hopis are familiar."[49] Dance societies from other pueblos
send groups of their supernaturals to take part in the general celebration.[50]
The Mudheads are always present; they entertain with crude and often
obscene play.

Dances are performed in all the kivas on the evening preceding the last
day of the ceremony. This is the occasion upon which the newly initiated
children learn, for the first time, that the kachina dancers whom they
have been taught to regard as supernatural beings are only mortal Hopis.
They sit with their mothers in the raised part of the kivas and watch the
Powamu Kachinas dance. These kachinas wear no masks, a rare occur-
rence for a formal dance night and one due, no doubt, to the presence
of the children. All the deities, both male and female, are impersonated
by men. The bodies of the male dancers are painted in the customary
bright colors: yellow on the left shoulder, the right forearm, and the left

PLATE 37. *Kokochi Dancer, Zuñi. One of the group of Rain Dancers, all of whom
wear the same costume.*   ⫸→

Plate 37

lower leg; blue-green on the right shoulder, the left forearm, and the right lower leg; white on the hands and the body from waist to knee; and red on the remaining parts. There are the usual white embroidered kilt, brocaded sash, red woven belt, and pendent foxskin. There are leg bands of dark blue wool, and a turtle-shell rattle behind the right knee. The moccasins are blue and red with wound heelpieces. A bandoleer of red and blue wool hangs over the right shoulder, and many strings of beads are around the neck. The gourd rattle is carried in the right hand and a spruce branch in the left. The hair hangs free, topped with an ornament of three cornhusk flowers (fig. 14, p. 87), and the face is rubbed with corn meal, which is said to absorb the perspiration.

The manas, or Maidens, are actually young men, each dressed in a woman's dark dress, red woven belt, and a maiden's blanket with red and blue borders, and wearing wrapped moccasins on feet and legs. There are strings of beads around the neck, and pendants hang from the ears. The hair is done in whorls, and a cornhusk sunflower is fastened to the forelock. A sprig of spruce is carried in the left hand. The face and arms are painted white with kaolin.[51]

At sunrise, on the last day, the sprouts of bean and corn, which had been planted early in the festival and forced to germinate by heating and watering, are tied into little bundles. Two men from each kiva, impersonating different kachinas, distribute them along with the kachina dolls and tiny bows and arrows which the men have made during the days of retreat. The bean sprouts are used as one of the dishes in the feast which terminates this long period of ceremony and festival.

CEREMONIAL KOKOCHI, ZUÑI

In the group dances in which the kachinas are all alike, the men are dressed with extreme care. Each part of a costume is as like that of its neighbor as human hand can make it. No corps de ballet in white tarlatan and pink slippers could be more uniform. The stiff white kilt is folded around the body to the same point above each knee, the shining black hair hangs to the same straight line at each waist, and the tail of each swinging foxskin clears the ground by the same few inches. The Zuñi Kokochi (pl. 37), the good or beautiful kachinas, are an excellent example of this nicety of similarity.

In September, 1936, I made a casual visit to the pueblo of Zuñi. Leaving my car near the road, I slowly circled the adobe houses in the direction of the sacred dance plaza. Suddenly I heard the deep tones of a chant, vibrant and somber. Climbing to the housetop, I looked down upon the dancing gods below. Forty-five dancers, facing each other, stretched in two lines along one side and part of each end of the plaza. One row, thirty-one in number, representing the male characters, danced shoulder to shoulder with their backs to the plaza. Nearest the wall and facing them were fourteen Kachina Maidens, who turned with the male dancers.[52] The movement flowed continuously from one end of the line to the other. Around, behind, and in the center capered the ten Mudheads, watching the dancers intently so that they might give immediate assistance when hair was entangled in evergreen sprig or turtle-shell rattle slipped from its leg position and interfered with a performer's movements. A dancing god should be as unconscious of such irritating trifles as a West Point cadet on dress parade.

At the head of the lines stood the priest, without a mask, his gray hair clubbed at the neck and bound with a hairband, and a downy white eagle feather moving gently at his forelock. He wore a dark blue shirt of native weave with set-on sleeves, and a white kilt with a brocaded sash tied on the right side. On his legs were blue knitted leggings held in place by red and white garters. He carried a terraced-edged bowl from which he sprinkled meal to make a 'road', and a beautiful wand, the insigne of his society, made of many kinds of brilliant feathers fashioned together and concealing an ear of corn. This ear of corn is known as the "life token."

PLATE 38. *Kachina Maiden, Zuñi. Conventional dress of the female deities.*   ⟫→

Plate 38

In the long kachina line there were twenty-nine Kokochi, their bodies painted with pink clay from the Sacred Lake. Each one wore the conventional white embroidered kilt. The white plaited sash, the symbol of rain, was knotted on the right side and the long cord fringe moved restlessly with the dance. A red woven belt was looped over the sash. Pendent foxskins were fastened to the belts in the back, their tails clearing the ground by a scant three inches. Sprigs of spruce were stuck in each belt and woven into bristling anklets worn just above the bare feet. Spruce was carried in the left hand of each dancer. Just below each knee, bunches of dark blue native-spun yarn were tied. At the back of the right leg, just below the bend of the knee, was fastened the turtle-shell rattle. From it hung deer hoofs which hit against the hard shell as the uneven beat was accented with the right foot. A bunch of blue yarn ornamented the right wrist, and a bow guard of leather with silver and turquoise the left. Bunches of native blue yarn and many beautiful necklaces of turquoise and white shell were worn around the necks of the dancers. The right hand carried a gourd rattle filled with pebbles, the clatter of which simulated the sound of falling rain. The half masks were blue-green with rectangular black eyes. The added strip of leather edging the bottom was painted in blocks of black and white, "symbolic of the house of clouds" where the Sky Gods live.[53] A long beard hung from the lower edge of each mask. The dancer's own hair rippled loose and free with a knot of bright yellow parrot feathers on top of the head. A white homespun cotton cord, weighted with a piece of turquoise or a silver trinket, fell down the back, and to this at regular intervals downy eagle feathers had been attached in an erect position.

With the Kokochi, and dancing in their line, were two Upoyona or Cottonheads (pl. 17); one or two of whom often dance with the Kokochi.[54] They are gentle dancers, the sons of the chief of the sacred kachina village, and they occasionally come with the Kokochi to aid them in bringing rain.[55] They were dressed exactly the same as the other dancers: body paint, kilt, sash, belt, spruce sprigs, foxskins, and wrist guards, yarn on arms and legs, rattles. However, instead of spruce anklets they wore turquoise blue moccasins with red trim and black and white heelpieces of porcupine quill. Their helmet masks had blue faces, with domino-shaped designs around the eyeholes. There were large eartabs edged with thick fringes of hair, and the wigs were of black horsehair straight-bobbed at the lower edge of the great spruce collars. There were long, flat snouts, and topknots of downy white eagle and yellow parrot feathers, from which hung three strings of loosely twisted cotton cord laid over the black hair at the back.

The Kachina Maidens, or Kokwelashtoki (pl. 38), form the second line.[56] They wore black dresses of woven wool. White Hopi blankets with red and black borders were thrown over their shoulders. The feet were painted yellow and the hands white. The legs were covered with dark blue knitted leggings, and there were anklets of evergreens. Blue yarn was tied around the wrists, and bunches of spruce were in each hand. They also wore many necklaces. The half masks were white with rectangular black eyes, and the shiny blackness of the thick horsehair beard was broken by the soft whiteness of three long, downy, eagle feathers. The hair was parted in the middle and wound on either side over rectangular frames of wood; then it was bound with yarn. Thick black bangs of goat's wool hung completely around the head, thus concealing the edge of the mask. A single white downy eagle feather hung from the center of each forelock.[57]

The Kokochi Dance, a prayer for moisture, is performed more often than any other Zuñi ceremony. It always opens the summer series. It is especially important on the occasion of the return, every fourth year, from the Sacred Lake, where certain of the impersonators go to acquire clay and tortoises. The live tortoise is afterward carried in the dance. Later it is killed, and the shells are cleaned and made into dance rattles which

---

PLATE 39. *"Chiffoneti" clown, striped from neck to ankle.*   ⟫⟶

Plate 39

are worn by all masked dancers. These masked beings, "the prototype of the katcina,"[58] are particularly identified with the Lost Children. The legend says that in the course of wanderings subsequent to the mythical emergence of the Zuñi from the four worlds below, they crossed a stream. The children, carried upon the backs of their mothers, fell into the water and were immediately turned into snakes, turtles, lizards, and frogs.[59] Swimming into the Sacred Lake, they became kachinas, and they have lived there ever since. The manner of the Kokochi is always gentle and mild, and they always bring happiness to the people. Their prayers and dances call down the rains and thus keep the world green and beautiful. They come at any time in winter or summer and are impersonated by dancers from each of the kivas in turn. In winter, when the Kachina Maidens come to dance, they bring, hidden under their blankets, the corn for the people to plant in the spring. It is deposited on the altar of each kiva they visit, and the priest distributes it at the end of the dance ceremonial.

The Kokochi is one of the dances which "require the presence of a couple, male and female, at the head of the line, who go through certain peculiar motions and have certain esoteric prayers. Only three men know these prayers, and they must be invited to perform for all kivas."[60] The two lines form in the ceremonial chambers and march in order to the dance plaza. They are led by a priest who, scattering corn meal before them, "makes this their road."

These same masked dances are said to be found in other pueblos,[61] but nowhere is there such precision of step and unanimity of costume as in this oft-repeated Rain Dance of Zuñi.

CLOWNS

In its ceremonial organization every pueblo has at least traces of two esoteric orders of Clowns, the most potent of priest groups, who appear with the Kachinas and at the Rain Dances.[62] As "Delight Makers" they contribute the comedy interludes to the solemn religious dramas, and they also perform theatrical entertainments of a secular nature. These secret orders differ in name, membership, and duties in the various pueblos.

"Chiffoneti."—One order, the "Chiffoneti" (pl. 39), is called the Black Eyes at Taos and Isleta, Kossa among the Tewa, Koshare by the Keres, Tabösh at Jemez, Newekwe at Zuñi, and Paiakyamu at Hopi. The members of the different groups of this order impersonate, without the use of a mask, a certain kind of supernatural. For the concealment of their identities they depend entirely upon the painting of their bodies and faces and the arrangement of their hair and headdresses. These extraordinary beings are striped from head to foot in horizontal black and white earth colors. Their faces are white with circles of black around their mouths and eyes.* They wear breechclouts with the ends hanging to mid-thigh.[63] These are held in place by a narrow belt around the middle. The hair is parted in the center and bound in two bunches which stand upright on each side of the head and are trimmed with bristling rosettes of cornhusks.[64] Among the Tewa, this cornhusk is called "mist."[65] Short hair necessitates a two-pointed cap in imitation of the horned hairdress. This cap is striped in black and white, carrying out the general decorative scheme. Sometimes strips of black cloth are tied around the neck and knees. Branches of evergreen are worn in the belt, or in a bandoleer over the right shoulder,[66] or carried in the hands.[67]

The comic action of these entertainers is impromptu, and it occurs between the appearances of the main drama dance. For subject matter they make use of incidents in village gossip, or they mimic spectators in the crowd. Erna Fergusson, speaking of the Koshare at a Santo Domingo Tablita Dance, says that "a fat one, one day, caught sight of a plumpish matron watching the dance. She was trim and erect, and with a dignity that would have abashed any white clown. But not the Indian. Approaching her, in her full sight and knowledge, he minced, swinging his ample

---

* In one group, at Jemez, yellow and white body stripes are used (Parsons, 1925*b*, p. 91). The Newekwe at Zuñi are not all striped; some are merely "ash-colored," but their hair is done in the same manner (Stevenson, 1904, p. 436).

hips, extending a condescending hand, caricatured her so exactly, but with such complete good humor, that the dowager herself laughed and made friends."[68]

Again, these black and white clowns may entertain a crowd by dramatizing an incident. At Taos, on St. Geronimo's Day, a greased pole is set up in the middle of the plaza. From the top a sheep and various other spoils are hung, a reward for the one who successfully climbs that high. On a particular occasion, "one of the Delight Makers walked up under the pole on which the sheep was hanging and made sheep tracks with his fingers in the dust. . . . Another strolled by and, discovering sheep tracks, began trailing the animals eagerly, looking everywhere until, glancing up, the dangling sheep caught his eye. Then with tiny bows and arrows the actors began shooting at the sheep with great glee and horseplay. Afterwards they went through the performance of climbing the pole. When the first man slipped down they put earth on the shaft, and when he climbed part way the others dropped on all fours, acting the part of furious bulls . . . to discourage the climber's descent."[69]

When the influence of the Church made itself felt among the Rio Grande villages, many Catholic ceremonies[70] were burlesqued. This would indicate that in prehistoric times the 'play' was also about local matters, such as a caricature of some secret ritual which had been performed previously in the kiva.[71]

Mudheads.—Of the many groups comprising the second order of clown priests, the Mudheads (pl. 40) are the most active. Known locally at Zuñi as Koyemshi, and among the Hopi as Tachuki, they entertain between the dances with comic and often obscene interludes, or play their favorite games of beanbag, tag, and leapfrog, to the great interest and amusement of the spectators on the housetops. Representing childish, immature characters[72] in both action and appearance, they wear knobbed, soft masks of cotton cloth colored with pink clay from the Sacred Lake. The knobs, in various distorted shapes, are filled with raw cotton, seeds,[73] and earth from the footprints made by the inhabitants in the streets around the pueblo. By using this earth, the Mudheads are supposed to acquire a magical power over the people and can demand from them respect and reverence.[74] Sometimes feathers flutter from the knobs. The lower border of the mask is finished with a strip of black homespun tied at the throat. Concealed under this is a small bag of seeds from the native crops: squash, corn, and gourd. The body is painted all over with the sacred pink clay, and the only garment is a short kilt of black native cloth. The leader often wears a scant tunic caught over the right shoulder, and he is distinguished by this. At Zuñi this group always comes in a full company of ten representing brothers of one family,[75] but each member of the group has a different personality which is discernible in the expression on his welted face and by the antics he performs.

These Mudheads play an important part, as illustrated by Mr. Fewkes,[76] in a "theatrical performance" enacted at Hopi. In March the drama of the Plumed Serpent is performed by various groups not ceremonially related. On one of the evenings a series of several acts of the drama makes the rounds of the various kivas, at which the members of each clan are assembled. The principal theme of this drama centers about the mythical Great Serpents, symbolizing wind and flood, who come from the sky or from holes in the earth. The Serpents destroy the corn and other provender of the human race. The Spirits of the Ancients, the Mudheads, with superhuman powers which cause the corn to grow, struggle with these monsters in an attempt to overcome their destructive forces.

When these scenes are performed at the kivas, the audience sits at the raised end. In the middle of the room two men tend the fire which is the only source of light. Upon hearing the first group of actors at the hatchway above, these fire tenders rise and hold their blankets about the fire in order to darken the room. Behind this 'curtain' the scene is set. Some

PLATE 40. *Mudheads, clowns best known at Zuñi and Hopi. Grotesque and potent rain priests with bag mask and bull-roarer.*   》》→

Plate 40

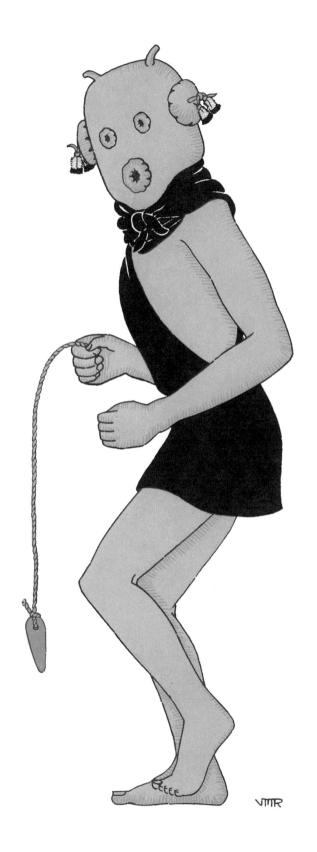

of the backgrounds are large screens of thick cotton cloth painted with symbolic designs of rainbows, clouds, and lightning. There is a row of circular holes covered by disks of deerskin with borders of plaited corn-husks. Through these holes, Serpent effigies, made of cloth with gourd heads,[77] are thrust to squirm and wriggle. The Serpents eventually sweep over a miniature cornfield and knock down the green sprouts set in clay balls in front of the screen. In one of the scenes the Serpents struggle with the ugly masked spirits who attempt to thwart their movements. In another scene two large jars are used, the effigies emerging from the tops as if from the earth.

These Serpent acts are interspersed with dances by masked figures and with interludes which deal with the Corn Maidens and the grinding of the corn into meal. The latter scene is sometimes enacted by marionettes, set in wooden frames and manipulated, as were the Serpents, by men concealed behind the screen.

The main purpose of this series of scenes is to instruct and entertain. Based upon legendary events, a combination of history and myth, they originated from ceremonial procedure, but they employ few of the sacred objects generally found in Hopi rites. Mr. Fewkes believes that these facts justify the application to them of the title, "theatrical exhibitions."

This mythical Serpent phase is found in other pueblos,[78] but at no other village has the ceremonial procedure given way to so secular a performance.

The scope of theatrical entertainment among the Pueblo Indians includes all these phases which appear between the simple, physical prayer, danced to climax a period of ritual and worship, and the pseudoreligious drama which has character impersonations and paraphernalia of ceremonial origin, but which disregards the demands of a patterned form.

As a phase of theatrical practice, the native Pueblo drama had its origin in the worship of supernatural powers and its development in the coercing of those powers and the instruction of its followers through story, impersonation, and action. It had approached the sphere of religious drama. Its death knell was sounded when an invading culture corrupted its beliefs and perverted its believers. Today the surviving practices indicate little of what might have been the full flowering of its maturity.

APPENDIX

PUEBLO LINGUISTIC GROUPS

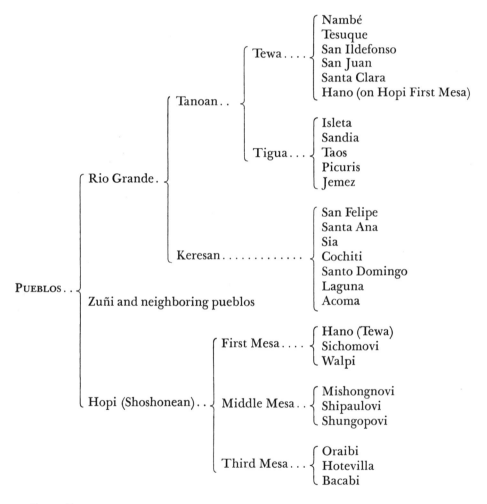

Pueblos..
- Rio Grande.
  - Tanoan..
    - Tewa....
      - Nambé
      - Tesuque
      - San Ildefonso
      - San Juan
      - Santa Clara
      - Hano (on Hopi First Mesa)
    - Tigua....
      - Isleta
      - Sandia
      - Taos
      - Picuris
      - Jemez
  - Keresan............
    - San Felipe
    - Santa Ana
    - Sia
    - Cochiti
    - Santo Domingo
    - Laguna
    - Acoma
- Zuñi and neighboring pueblos
- Hopi (Shoshonean)..
  - First Mesa....
    - Hano (Tewa)
    - Sichomovi
    - Walpi
  - Middle Mesa..
    - Mishongnovi
    - Shipaulovi
    - Shungopovi
  - Third Mesa...
    - Oraibi
    - Hotevilla
    - Bacabi

Notes

NOTE: Bibliographical references are abbreviated to author's name, date of publication, and page of work cited. This forms a key to the full titles given in the Bibliography, pages 247–251.

NOTES

PART ONE

THE PUEBLOS, THEIR HISTORY AND PRESENT LIFE

[1] Goddard, 1931:23 ff. and 63 ff.; Douglas, 1930c, 1930d.
[2] Luxàn, 1929:98.
[3] Winship, 1894; Hodge, 1895: 149.
[4] Harrington, 1916:37.
[5] Beals, 1935:10.
[6] Beals, 1935:31.
[7] Parsons, 1925a:74.
[8] Goldfrank, 1927:93.
[9] Beals, 1935:10.
[10] Bunzel, 1929.
[11] Stevenson, 1904:193.
[12] Hough, 1919:251.
[13] Parsons, 1936a:26.
[14] Parsons, 1925a:111, 113.
[15] Benedict, 1928:577.
[16] Bunzel, 1932a:480.
[17] Beals, 1935:43.
[18] Parsons, 1924:140.
[19] Benedict, 1928:573.
[20] Hewett, 1930:74.
[21] Hewett, 1930:74.
[22] Beals, 1935:45; Parsons, 1924: 146.
[23] Beals, 1935:45.
[24] Bunzel, 1932a:478.
[25] Bunzel, 1932d:877.
[26] Parsons, 1925a:31, 43.
[27] Goddard, 1931:79.
[28] Bunzel, 1932d:877.
[29] White, 1932a:31.
[30] Parsons, 1929:100.
[31] Parsons, 1932:209.
[32] Bunzel, 1932a:493.
[33] Davis, 1929:264. General Davis undoubtedly describes such a mask which he saw in the summer of 1865.
[34] White, 1935:89.
[35] Bunzel, 1932d:843.
[36] Beals, 1935:40.
[37] White, 1932a:69.
[38] Bunzel, 1932a:517.
[39] Bunzel, 1932b:607; 1932a:517.
[40] White, 1932a:69, 148.
[41] Bunzel, 1932a:517.
[42] Parsons, 1933:40.
[43] Hough, 1915:132.
[44] Spinden, 1915:113–115.
[45] Bunzel, 1932d:886.
[46] Spinden, 1915:108.
[47] Lowie, 1915:96.
[48] Bunzel, 1932a:495.
[49] Hewett, 1924:117.
[50] Hewett, 1936:235.
[51] Hodge, 1925:23.
[52] Parsons, 1925b:6.

PART TWO

COSTUME MATERIALS AND THEIR SIGNIFICANCE

[1] Amsden, 1934:2.
[2] Amsden, 1934:4.
[3] Matthews, 1884:375.
[4] Robbins *et al.*, 1916:52.
[5] Spier, 1924:65.
[6] McGregor, 1931.
[7] Wissler, 1922:43.
[8] Winship, 1896:570, 587.
[9] Colton, 1930.
[10] Hough, 1919:262, 281.
[11] Lewton, 1912:9; McGregor, 1931.
[12] James, 1914:12.
[13] Spier, 1924:64.
[14] Lewton, 1912:7.
[15] Cf. Amsden, 1934:pl. x.
[16] Douglas, 1933a.
[17] Amsden, 1934:21; Crawford, 1931:31, 33.
[18] Spier, 1924:66 ff.; Amsden, 1934:37; Colton, 1931; Douglas, 1931.
[19] Spier, 1924:74, a detailed account of belt weaving.
[20] Amsden, 1934:52–53.
[21] Amsden, 1934:57; Colton, 1930; Hough, 1919:258; Bartlett, 1936.
[22] Spier, 1924:80.
[23] Stevenson, 1883:434.
[24] Bartlett, 1936.
[25] Winship, 1896:586.
[26] Henderson and Harrington, 1914:5.
[27] Winship, 1896:516–518.
[28] Dumarest, 1919:235.
[29] Goddard, 1931:131, 155.
[30] Dumarest, 1919, 168.
[31] Goldfrank, 1927:82.
[32] Winship, 1896:527, 578; Steece, 1931:414.
[33] Goddard, 1931:155.
[34] Bunzel, 1932d:pl. 25a.
[35] Douglas, 1930a.
[36] Catlin, 1857:44.
[37] Douglas, 1930a.
[38] Catlin, 1857:45; Hiler, 1929:142.
[39] Henderson, 1931:15.
[40] Hiler, 1929:109, 138.
[41] Stevenson, 1904:114.
[42] Parsons, 1936a:38; 1920a:100; 1921:154; 1932:352; White, 1932a:36; 1932b:21; Stevenson, 1904:292.
[43] Stevenson, 1915:89.
[44] White, 1932a:75 ff.
[45] Fewkes, 1903:32; Henderson and Harrington, 1914:45.
[46] Bunzel, 1932d:863.
[47] Parsons, 1932:274; 1925b:104; Bunzel, 1932a:500.
[48] Henderson and Harrington, 1914:34–36.
[49] Winship, 1896:520.
[50] Goddard, 1931:89.
[51] Parsons, 1932:291.
[52] Stevenson, 1904:pl. CXXIII.
[53] Dumarest, 1919:172.
[54] Fewkes, 1903:67.
[55] Bunzel, 1932a:867.
[56] Bunzel, 1932c:660.
[57] Dumarest, 1919:156; Parsons, 1920a:125; 1920b:62.
[58] Dumarest, 1919:156.
[59] Peet, 1894:350.
[60] Dumarest, 1919:194.
[61] Fewkes, 1900a.
[62] Stevenson, 1904:114.
[63] Winship, 1896:516.
[64] Dumarest, 1919:146 n.; Bunzel, 1932d:863 n.

[65] Dumarest, 1919:146 n.
[66] Dumarest, 1919:166 n. 2.
[67] Bunzel, 1932*d*:988, 994.
[68] Frazer, 1935:202.
[69] Bunzel, 1932*a*:500.
[70] Bunzel, 1932*c*:600.
[71] Parsons, 1925*b*:15.
[72] Bunzel, 1932*d*:863.
[73] Parsons, 1932:262.
[74] Bunzel, 1932*a*, 418.
[75] Dumarest, 1919:216 n.
[76] Bunzel, 1932*a*:500.
[77] Bunzel, 1932*d*:1046.
[78] Parsons, 1925*b*:104.
[79] Basket Dancers, Yale Collection, T. d. 6A. 185, 186.
[80] Parsons, 1925*b*:104.
[81] Rio Grande exhibit, Museum of Natural History, New York.
[82] Stevenson, 1915:36.
[83] Stevenson, 1915:97.
[84] Robbins *et al.*, 1916:43.
[85] Yale Collection, T. e. 6A. 58, 59, 60, 61, 62.
[86] Fewkes, 1903:51; Parsons, 1936*b*: 291 ff.; Stevenson, 1904:94; Yale Collection, T. g. 6A. 1.
[87] Stevenson, 1915:88.
[88] Bunzel, 1932*d*:842.
[89] Bunzel, 1932*a*:506; White, 1932*a*:132; Parsons, 1932:262.
[90] Exhibit, Brooklyn Museum.
[91] Stevenson, 1915:100.
[92] Hough, 1919:259.
[93] Parsons, 1920*a*:99.
[94] Fergusson, 1931:130.
[95] Stevenson, 1915:92.
[96] Hiler, 1929:139.
[97] Dixon, 1899:10.
[98] Bunzel, 1932*d*:862.
[99] Bunzel, 1932*d*:989.
[100] Stevenson, 1904:244.
[101] Bunzel, 1932*d*:988.
[102] Dumarest, 1919:181 n.
[103] Bunzel, 1932*d*:862.
[104] Bunzel, 1932*d*:1006.
[105] McGregor, 1931.
[106] Bunzel, 1932*d*:861.
[107] Parsons, 1925*b*:16.
[108] White, 1932*a*:131.
[109] Douglas, 1933*b*.
[110] Bunzel, 1932*d*:859.
[111] Bunzel, 1932*d*:860; White, 1932*b*:29.
[112] Robbins *et al.*, 1916:51.
[113] Dumarest, 1919:199.
[114] White, 1932*a*:131.
[115] Fewkes, 1900*a*:691.
[116] White, 1932*a*:131.
[117] Parsons, 1929:248.
[118] Bunzel, 1932*d*:859.
[119] Dumarest, 1919:199; Parsons, 1920*b*:58; 1921:157.
[120] Bunzel, 1932*d*:860.
[121] Parsons, 1925*b*:112.
[122] Dumarest, 1919:199; White, 1932*a*:131.
[123] Robbins *et al.*, 1916:49.
[124] Bunzel, 1932*d*:860; Parsons, 1925*b*:112.
[125] Parsons, 1929:248.
[126] Parsons, 1925*b*:112. Cf. exhibit, Museum of the American Indian, Heye Foundation, New York; Yale Collection, T. e. 6A. 54, 55.
[127] Bunzel, 1932*d*:806.
[128] White, 1932*a*:131; Dumarest, 1919:184; Parsons, 1920*a*:101, 109; 1932:320; Bunzel, 1932*a*: 860.
[129] Dallenbaugh, 1933:85.
[130] Bunzel, 1932*d*:860.
[131] Parsons, 1920*a*:128.
[132] Bunzel, 1923*d*:861.
[133] White, 1932*a*:131.
[134] Bunzel, 1932*d*:860.
[135] Douglas, 1934.
[136] Robbins *et al.*, 1916:39.
[137] Hough, 1897:40.
[138] See Amsden, 1934:87–93, for a detailed description of Navaho dyes.
[139] Douglas, 1931.

[140] Colton, 1933:49.
[141] New Mexico Association of Indian Affairs, 1936.
[142] Kissel, 1931:15.
[143] Stevenson, 1904:pl. xciii.

[144] Douglas, 1930*b*.
[145] Aitken, 1924:96.
[146] Hough, 1919:260.
[147] Hough, 1919:263.
[148] Orchard, 1931:5.

PART THREE

DETAILED ANALYSES OF PARTS OF COSTUMES

[1] Hiler, 1929:65.
[2] Hiler, 1929:12.
[3] Bunzel, 1932*d*:868.
[4] Bunzel, 1932*d*:869.
[5] Keech, 1933:190–192.
[6] Bunzel, 1932*d*:pl. 28.
[7] Bunzel, 1932*d*:868.
[8] Hewett, 1922:105, fig. 2.
[9] Parsons, 1929:193.
[10] Hartley, 1919:54.
[11] Bunzel, 1932*d*:868.
[12] Dumarest, 1919:184 n. 7.
[13] See myth *Uretsete*, Dumarest, 1919:212 ff.
[14] Colton, 1933.
[15] Hough, 1919:250.
[16] Yale Collection, T. d. 6A. 2036.
[17] Hough, 1919:257.
[18] Yale Collection, T. d. 6A. 136.
[19] Stevenson, unpublished MS.
[20] Douglas, 1930*b*.
[21] Yale Collection, T. d. 6A. 8.
[22] Bunzel, 1932*d*:948.
[23] From Cushing's emergence myth, Bunzel, 1932*d*:949.
[24] Douglas, 1930*b*.
[25] Bunzel, 1932*d*:869.
[26] Yale Collection, T. d. 6A. 2034.
[27] Hough, 1919:257.
[28] Peet, 1894:355.
[29] Yale Collection, T. d. 6A. 187.
[30] Yale Collection, T. d. 6A. 112.
[31] Bunzel, 1932*d*:989.
[32] Bunzel, 1932*d*:pl. 30.

[33] Yale Collection, T. d. 6A. 137.
[34] Yale Collection, T. d. 6A. 64.
[35] Alexander, 1926:317.
[36] Yale Collection, T. d. 6A. 8.
[37] Spinden, 1915:113–114, illustrations.
[38] Hough, 1919:242.
[39] Douglas, 1931.
[40] Spier, 1924:70.
[41] Douglas, 1930*b*.
[42] Douglas, 1930*b*.
[43] Parsons, 1936*a*:26.
[44] Stevenson, 1904:371; also unpublished MS:127; Douglas, 1931; Stevenson, 1884:398.
[45] Hough, 1919:243, fig. 14; Stevenson, 1884:594.
[46] Bunzel, 1932*d*:870.
[47] Keech, 1933:190; 1934*a*:129.
[48] Hough, 1919:251.
[49] Stevenson, 1904:371.
[50] Parsons, 1925*b*:18.
[51] Parsons, 1936*a*:25.
[52] Bunzel, 1932*d*:861.
[53] Stevenson, 1884:fig. 579.
[54] Hough, 1919:258.
[55] Stevenson, 1884:fig. 582.
[56] Information gained through correspondence with Frederic H. Douglas, Curator of the Denver Art Museum.
[57] Hough, 1919:259.
[58] Hough, 1919:255.
[59] Hough, 1919:257.

[60] Hewett, 1924:208.
[61] Yale Collection, T. d. 6A. 17.
[62] Bunzel, 1932*d*:870; 1932*b*:584, 591.
[63] Yale Collection, T. d. 6A. 118, 126.
[64] Yale Collection, T. d. 6A. 122.
[65] Keech, 1933:190; 1934*a*:147; Parsons, 1925*b*:113.
[66] Bunzel, 1932*d*:871; Yale Collection, T. d. 6A. 8.
[67] Yale Collection, T. d. 6A. 111, 116, 121.
[68] Bunzel, 1932*d*:871.
[69] Stevenson, 1884:565.
[70] Winship, 1896:549.
[71] Bunzel, 1932*d*:871 n. 31.
[72] Douglas, 1932.
[73] Sloan and La Farge, 1931:33.
[74] Sloan and La Farge, 1931:37.
[75] Bunzel, 1932*d*:871.
[76] Voth, 1901:pl. xxix; Parsons, 1932:355.
[77] Hough, 1919:293.
[78] Stevenson, 1904:pl. LXXXI.
[79] Hough, 1919:fig. 45; Voth, 1901:pl. LXVIII.
[80] Exhibit, Brooklyn Museum.
[81] Robbins *et al.*, 1916:102.
[82] Hopi *Marau Ba'ho* (ceremonial tablet wand), Museum of Natural History, New York.
[83] Stevenson, 1904:186.

[84] Hewett, 1924:212.
[85] Chapman, 1925:45.
[86] Parsons, 1936*a*:26.
[87] Dumarest, 1919:186 n.
[88] Bunzel, 1932*d*:868.
[89] Stevenson, 1904:pl. XXXVIII.
[90] Fewkes, 1910:588.
[91] Fewkes, 1910:577.
[92] MacGowan and Rosse, 1923: introd., xi.
[93] Stevenson, 1904:33.
[94] MacGowan and Rosse, 1923:95.
[95] Dorsey and Voth, 1901: pl. XXVII.
[96] Yale Collection, T. d. 6A. 157.
[97] Yale Collection, T. e. 6A. 4, 25.
[98] Yale Collection, T. e. 6A. 65, 66.
[99] Douglas, 1935.
[100] Bunzel, 1932*d*:849 ff.
[101] Yale Collection, T. e. 6A. 56.
[102] Yale Collection, T. e. 6A. 69–70.
[103] Yale Collection, T. e. 6A. 51.
[104] Yale Collection, T. e. 6A. 73.
[105] Bunzel, 1932*d*:990.
[106] Bunzel, 1932*d*:988.
[107] Bunzel, 1932*d*:864.
[108] Parsons, 1925*b*:112.
[109] Bunzel, 1932*d*:848.
[110] Dall, 1884:93.
[111] Stevenson, 1904:250.
[112] Yale Collection, T. e. 6A. 78.
[113] Cf. Fewkes, 1903: pl. LVI.
[114] Fewkes, 1903:119.

PART FOUR

COSTUMES IN RELATION TO THE PRAYER DRAMA

[1] Fewkes, 1894:43.
[2] Fewkes, 1894:40–47.
[3] Fewkes, 1903:15.
[4] Parsons, 1925*b*:113; 1919:34–38; White, 1932*a*:131; Goldfrank, 1927:63; Keech, 1933:194.

[5] Goldfrank, 1927:108.
[6] Parsons, 1929:107.
[7] Parsons, 1929:123.
[8] Parsons, 1929:pls. 21, 22.
[9] Bunzel, 1932*d*:902.
[10] Parsons, 1929:195.

[11] Parsons, 1936a:93.

[12] Parsons, 1929:pl. II.

[13] Parsons, 1929:187.

[14] An early example of this head-dress is exhibited in the American Museum of Natural History, New York.

[15] A report of this dance was made by Parsons, 1929:200.

[16] See sketch, "San Ildefonso Animal Dance," by Awa Tsirah, in Alexander, 1932:pl. xxx.

[17] White, 1932b:57 n.

[18] Parsons, 1929:205 f.

[19] Parsons, 1929:sketch opp. p. 12.

[20] Bunzel, 1932d:1067.

[21] Fewkes, 1903:77.

[22] Bunzel, 1932d:1068 f.

[23] Parsons, 1936a:88.

[24] Parsons, 1936a:89.

[25] Alexander, 1932:pl. 16.

[26] Parsons, 1924:111.

[27] Bunzel, 1932d:1041.

[28] Fewkes, 1903:103.

[29] Parsons, 1922:206.

[30] Parsons, 1925b:pls. 14, 17.

[31] Fewkes, 1903:17.

[32] Fewkes, 1903:22.

[33] Fewkes, 1903:31.

[34] Fewkes, 1897:274.

[35] Fewkes, 1903:32.

[36] Fewkes, 1897:279.

[37] Fewkes, 1903:33.

[38] Yale Collection, T. d. 6A. 72, 1086.

[39] Yale Collection, T. d. 6A. 4.

[40] Voth, 1901:110–112.

[41] Fewkes, 1897:281, pl. cvi.

[42] Fewkes, 1903:71; 1897:281, pl. cvi.

[43] Voth, 1901:94 ff.

[44] Fewkes, 1903:68; Voth, 1901:96.

[45] Voth, 1901:94.

[46] Voth has given Oraibi names to these characters because he ob-served the ceremony at Oraibi. For the sake of clarity I shall continue to use Walpi names assigned by Fewkes, 1903:36.

[47] Voth, 1901:pl. LII.

[48] Voth, 1901:98.

[49] Fewkes, 1903:17.

[50] Fewkes, 1903:36.

[51] Voth, 1901:121.

[52] Bunzel, 1932d:898.

[53] Stevenson, 1904:105.

[54] Bunzel, 1932d:1015.

[55] Parsons, 1922:192.

[56] Bunzel, 1932d:1013.

[57] Stevenson, 1904:104 f.

[58] Bunzel, 1932d:1013.

[59] Bunzel, 1932b:595.

[60] Bunzel, 1932d:897.

[61] Bunzel, 1932d:901, 1013.

[62] Spinden, 1915:108; Parsons, 1925b:91; Stevenson, 1904:436.

[63] Parsons, 1929:pls. 22, 26; Sloan and La Farge, 1931: pl. VI.

[64] Reagan, 1915:426.

[65] Parsons, 1929:126.

[66] Keech, 1934a:146.

[67] The Tabosh at Jemez wear garlands of yellow flowers, "two garlands are around the neck to cross over chest." Parsons, 1925b: 91.

[68] Fergusson, 1933:657.

[69] Bailey, 1924:92.

[70] Dumarest, 1919:185; Parsons, 1929:183.

[71] Parsons, 1929:92.

[72] Bunzel, 1932d:951.

[73] Bunzel, 1932d:946.

[74] Parsons, 1917:235.

[75] Bunzel, 1932d:948.

[76] Fewkes, 1900b:605–629.

[77] Fewkes, 1894:pls. 1 and 2.

[78] At Zuñi, Stevenson, 1904:94; among the Tewa, Parsons, 1929: 274.

Bibliography

BIBLIOGRAPHY

AITKEN, BARBARA

1924. A Tewa craftsman—Leslie Aga-yo. El Palacio, Vol. XVII.

ALEXANDER, HARTLEY BURR

1926. The rain cloud in Indian myth. El Palacio, XXI:317.

1932. Pueblo Indian Painting. (Nice, 1932)

AMSDEN, CHARLES AVERY

1934. Navaho Weaving. (Santa Ana, 1934)

BAILEY, FLORENCE M.

1924. Some plays and dances of the Taos Indians. Natural History, XXIV:92.

BARTLETT, KATHERINE

1936. How to appreciate Hopi handi-crafts. Museum of Northern Arizona, Museum Notes, Vol. IX, No. 2.

BEALS, RALPH L.

1935. Preliminary Report of the Ethnography of the Southwest. U. S. Department of the Interior, National Park Service. (Berkeley, 1935)

BENEDICT, RUTH

1928. Psychological types in the cultures of the Southwest. International Congress of Americanists, Proceedings, Vol. XXIII.

BUNZEL, RUTH

1929. The Pueblo potter. Columbia University, Contributions to Anthropology, Vol. VIII.

1932a. Introduction to Zuñi ceremonialism. Bureau of American Ethnology, Annual Reports, XLVII: 467–544.

1932b. Zuñi origin myths. Bureau of American Ethnology, Annual Reports, XLVII:545–610.

1932c. Zuñi ritual poetry. Bureau of American Ethnology, Annual Reports, XLVII:611–836.

1932d. Zuñi katcinas. Bureau of American Ethnology, Annual Reports, XLVII:837–1086.

CATLIN, GEORGE

1857. North American Indians. (London) Vol. I.

CHAPMAN, KATE M.

1925. Sun basket dance at Santa Clara. El Palacio, XVIII:45.

COLTON, MARY RUSSELL

1930. The Hopi craftsman. Museum of Northern Arizona, Museum Notes, Vol. III, No. 1.

1931. Techniques of the major Hopi crafts. Museum of Northern Arizona, Museum Notes, Vol. III, No. 12.

COLTON, MARY RUSSELL—*Continued*

1933. Hopi courtship and marriage. Museum of Northern Arizona, Museum Notes, Vol. V, No. 8.

CRAWFORD, M. D. C.

1931. The Heritage of Cotton. (New York, 1931)

DALL, WILLIAM HEALEY

1884. On masks, labrets, and certain aboriginal customs. Bureau of American Ethnology, Annual Reports, III:93.

DALLENBAUGH, FREDERICK S.

1933. Red paint. Southwest Museum, The Masterkey, Vol. VII.

DAVIS, W. W. H.

1929. The Pueblo Indians of New Mexico. El Palacio, XXVI:264.

DIXON, ROLAND B.

1899. The color symbolism of the cardinal points. Journal of American Folklore, Vol. XII.

DORSEY, GEORGE A., and VOTH, H. R.

1901. The Oraibi *soy'al* ceremony. Field Columbian Museum, Anthropological Series, III:1.

DOUGLAS, FREDERIC H.

1930a. Hide dressing and bead sewing techniques. Denver Art Museum, Leaflet 2.

1930b. Pueblo Indian clothing. Denver Art Museum, Leaflet 4.

1930c. Periods of Pueblo culture and history. Denver Art Museum, Leaflet 11.

1930d. The Pueblo Golden Age. Denver Art Museum, Leaflet 14.

1931. Hopi Indian weaving. Denver Art Museum, Leaflet 18.

1932. Pueblo beads and inlay. Denver Art Museum, Leaflet 30.

1933a. Navaho spinning, dyeing and weaving. Denver Art Museum, Leaflet 3 (2d edition).

1933b. Colors in Indian arts: their sources and uses. Denver Art Museum, Leaflet 56.

1934. Indian vegetable dyes. Denver Art Museum, Leaflet 63.

1935. Types of Indian masks. Denver Art Museum, Leaflets 65–66.

DUMAREST, NOEL

1919. Notes on Cochiti, New Mexico. American Anthropological Association, Memoirs, VI:139–236.

FERGUSSON, ERNA

1931. Dancing Gods. (New York, 1931)

1933. Laughing priests. Theatre Arts Monthly, XVII:657–662.

FEWKES, J. WALTER

1894. Dolls of the Tusayan Indians. Internationales Archiv für Ethnographie, VII:45–73.

1897. Tusayan katcinas. Bureau of American Ethnology, Annual Reports, XV:251–320.

1900a. Property rights in eagles among the Hopi. American Anthropologist, II:690–707.

1900b. A theatrical performance at Walpi. Washington Academy of Science, Proceedings, II:605–629.

1903. Hopi katcinas. Bureau of American Ethnology, Annual Reports, Vol. XXI.

1910. The butterfly in Hopi myth and ritual. American Anthropologist, XII:577.

FEWKES, J. WALTER, and STEPHEN, A. M.

1893. The Pa'-lü-lü-koñ-ti: a Tusayan ceremony. Journal of American Folklore, VI:269–282.

FRAZER, SIR JAMES GEORGE
1935. The Golden Bough. (New York) Vol. XI.

GODDARD, PLINY E.
1931. Indians of the Southwest. American Museum of Natural History, Handbook Series, Vol. II.

GOLDFRANK, ESTHER SCHIFF
1927. The social and ceremonial organization of Cochiti. American Anthropological Association, Memoirs, Vol. XXXIII.

HARRINGTON, J. P.
1916. The ethnogeography of the Tewa Indians. Bureau of American Ethnology, Annual Reports, XXIX:29–618.

HARTLEY, MARSDEN
1919. Tribal esthetics, dance drama. El Palacio, VI:54.

HENDERSON, EARL Y.
1931. The Havasupai Indian Agency, Arizona. Department of the Interior, Office of Indian Affairs.

HENDERSON, JUNIUS, and HARRINGTON, JOHN PEABODY
1914. Ethnozoölogy of the Tewa Indians. Bureau of American Ethnology, Bulletin LVI.

HEWETT, EDGAR L.
1922. Native American artist. Art and Archaeology, XIII:103–119.

1924. Indian ceremonies. El Palacio, Vol. XVII.

1930. Ancient Life in the American Southwest. (Indianapolis)

1936. Ancient Life in Mexico and Central America. (New York)

HILER, HILAIRE
1929. From Nudity to Raiment. (London)

HODGE, F. W.
1895. The first discovered city of Cibola. American Anthropologist, old series, VIII:142.

1925. Rites of the Pueblo Indians. El Palacio, XVIII:23–28.

1937. History of Hawikuh, New Mexico. (Los Angeles)

HOUGH, WALTER
1897. The Hopi in relation to their plant environment. American Anthropologist, old series, Vol. X.

1902. The Moki Snake Dance. (Santa Fe)

1915. The Hopi Indians. (Cedar Rapids)

1919. The Hopi Indian collection in the United States National Museum. United States National Museum, Proceedings, LIV:235–297.

JAMES, GEORGE WHARTON
1914. Indian Blankets and Their Makers. (Chicago)

KEECH, ROY A.
1933. Two days and nights in a pueblo. El Palacio, XXXV:190.

1934a. Green corn ceremony at the Pueblo of Zia, 1932. El Palacio, XXXVI:146.

1934b. Pecos ceremony at Jemez, August 2, 1932. El Palacio, XXXVI:129.

KISSEL, MARY L.
1931. Indian weaving. Introduction to American Indian Art, II:15–21.

LEWTON, FREDERICK L.
1912. Cotton of the Hopi Indians. Smithsonian Miscellaneous Collections, LX:4.

LOWIE, ROBERT H.

1915. American Indian dances. American Museum Journal, Vol. XV.

LUXÁN, DIEGO PÉREZ DE

1929. Expedition into New Mexico Made by Antonio de Espejo, 1582–1583. Translated by George Peter Hammond and Agapito Rey. (Los Angeles, 1929)

MACGOWAN, KENNETH, and ROSSE, HERMAN

1923. Masks and Demons. (New York)

MCGREGOR, J. C.

1931. Prehistoric cotton fabric of Arizona. Museum of Northern Arizona, Museum Notes, Vol. IV, No. 2.

MATTHEWS, WASHINGTON

1884. Navajo weavers. Bureau of American Ethnology, Annual Reports, III:371–391.

NEW MEXICO ASSOCIATION OF INDIAN AFFAIRS

1936. Indian Art Series, No. 3.

ORCHARD, WILLIAM C.

1931. Indian porcupine quill and bead work. Introduction to American Indian Art, II:3–13.

PARSONS, ELSIE CLEWS

1917. Notes on Zuñi. Part II. American Anthropological Association, Memoirs, IV:229–327.

1919. Mothers and children at Laguna. Man, XIX:34–38.

1920a. Notes on ceremonialism at Laguna. American Museum of Natural History, Anthropological Papers, XIX:92–132.

1920b. Notes on Isleta, Santa Ana, and Acoma. American Anthropologist, XX:56–69.

1921. Further notes on Isleta. American Anthropologist, XXIII:149–169.

1922. Winter and summer dance series in Zuñi in 1918. University of California, Publications in American Archaeology and Ethnology, XVII:171–216.

1924. The religion of the Pueblo Indians. International Congress of Americanists, Proceedings, XXI:140–161.

1925a. A Pueblo Indian journal. American Anthropological Association, Memoirs, Vol. XXXII.

1925b. The Pueblo of Jemez. (New Haven, 1925)

1929. The social organization of the Tewa of New Mexico. American Anthropological Association, Memoirs, Vol. XXXVI.

1932. Isleta, New Mexico. Bureau of American Ethnology, Annual Reports, XLVII:193–466.

1933. Hopi and Zuñi ceremonialism. American Anthropological Association, Memoirs, Vol. XXXIX.

1936a. Taos Pueblo. General Series in Anthropology, Vol. II.

1936b. Hopi journal of Alexander M. Stephen. Columbia University, Contributions to Anthropology, Vol. XXIII.

PEET, STEPHEN D.

1894. The worship of the rain-god. American Antiquarian and Oriental Journal, Vol. XVI:341–356.

REAGAN, ALBERT

1915. Masked dances. Southern Workmen, Vol. XLIV.

ROBBINS, WILFRED W., HARRINGTON, JOHN PEABODY, and FREIRE-MARRECO, BARBARA

1916. Ethnobotany of the Tewa Indians. Bureau of American Ethnology, Bulletin LV.

SLOAN, JOHN, and LA FARGE, OLIVER

1931. Introduction to American Indian Art. (New York, 1931) Vol. I.

SPIER, LESLIE

1924. Zuñi weaving technique. American Anthropologist, XXVI:64–85.

SPINDEN, HERBERT J.

1915. Indian dances of the Southwest. American Museum Journal, Vol. XV.

STEECE, HENRY M.

1931. Corn culture among the Indians of the Southwest. Natural History, Vol. XXI.

STEVENSON, JAMES

1883. Collection of 1880. Bureau of American Ethnology, Annual Reports, II:429–465.

1884. Collection of 1881. Bureau of American Ethnology, Annual Reports, III:511–594.

STEVENSON, MATILDA C.

1904. The Zuñi Indians. Bureau of American Ethnology, Annual Reports, XXIII:1–608.

1915. Ethnobotany of the Zuñi Indians. Bureau of American Ethnology, Annual Reports, XXX: 31–102.

—— Unpublished MS, Smithsonian Institute, Washington, D. C.

VOTH, H. R.

1901. The Oraibi *po wa mu* ceremony. Field Museum of Natural History, Anthropological Series, III:67–158.

WHITE, LESLIE A.

1932a. The Acoma Indians. Bureau of American Ethnology, Annual Reports, XLVII:17–192.

1932b. The Pueblo of San Felipe. American Anthropological Association, Memoirs, XXXVIII:5–70.

1935. The pueblo of Santo Domingo, New Mexico. American Anthropologist, Vol. XLIII.

WINSHIP, GEORGE PARKER

1894. Coronado's journey to New Mexico and the Great Plains. Translated from the Spanish. American History Leaflets, No. XIII.

1896. The Coronado Expedition, 1540–1542. Bureau of American Ethnology, Annual Reports, XLV: 329–613.

WISSLER, CLARK

1922. The American Indian. (New York, 1922)

Yale Theatre Collection, Department of Drama, Yale University, New Haven. (Photographs of material in various museums and private collections gathered together for purposes of comparison and study.)

COMPOSITION, PRESSWORK AND BINDING OF THIS BOOK
HAVE BEEN DONE BY THE UNIVERSITY OF CALIFORNIA PRESS, BERKELEY
DESIGNED BY SAMUEL T. FARQUAHAR AND A. R. TOMMASINI
COLOR PLATES PRINTED FROM RUBBER BLOCKS
CUT BY HAND BY JEAN GOODWIN AND ARTHUR AMES. COMPOSITION
SUPERVISED BY A. R. TOMMASINI, PRESSWORK BY A. J. EVANS
AND BINDING BY A. W. HALLING

THE ABOVE COLOPHON APPEARED IN THE FIRST EDITION IN 1941.
THIS EDITION WAS REPRODUCED FROM THE ORIGINAL WITH
ADDITIONAL COMPOSITION IN MATCHING MONOTYPE
BASKERVILLE BY M & H TYPE OF SAN FRANCISCO.
COLOR SEPARATIONS, PRINTING AND BINDING
BY DAI NIPPON (AMERICA) INC.
THE PAPER IS KINMARY V,
157 GSM.
JACKET AND COVER DESIGN BY
STEVE RENICK.
PRINTED AND BOUND IN
HONG KONG.